MW00576235

Comments from Readers

Note that quotes marked with an asterisk reference
the first version of the curriculum, which was titled
Abstinence Because of Love.

"*The True Love Thing to Do* is a great tool for a much needed, open, and frank discussion about love, sex, and marriage. It is practical, useful, and based on solid principles. It is also an excellent book for parents to assist them in giving guidance to their children about these topics."

> Pastor Darwin Vail,
> Pastor Emeritus,
> Bible Believing Baptist Church

"This booklet is a must-read for those who want to learn a positive way to promote what for some has become a negative concept . . . Abstinence! 'Love' is such a warm and fuzzy word, but this booklet will help you realize that true love will always demand sacrifice. To love someone enough to want the best for them, spiritually, emotionally, and physically, will involve hard work! To say no to sex outside of marriage is saying, 'I want the best for you and the best for myself,' and it can be difficult to do, but it will be so rewarding! Reward yourself and read *Abstinence Because of Love*." *

> Molly Kelly, national lecturer on chastity
> and a huge fan of today's teens!

"Today's society bombards young people with messages that confuse sex with true love. *Abstinence Because of Love* will help young people understand that true love, as defined by respect and lifelong commitment, is the key to long-term sexual and emotional fulfillment." *
                                 Shepherd Smith
                                 Institute for Youth Development

"Any young person who wants to build happiness in his or her life will find priceless wisdom in this book about the ways and means of true love."
                                 Clark Eberly, Research Librarian
                                 Washington Times, 1982–2009

"Provides a clear, straightforward explanation of why abstinence and lasting love are interconnected."
                                 Richard Panzer, Founder of Free Teens

"Peter Brown has bravely tackled an important and difficult subject. It is a work that lives up to its stated goal of 'examining life with an active mind.' More importantly, the love and concern that have been infused into his writing come through clearly and in abundance."
                                 Daniel K. Berman, PhD
                                 Harvard graduate
                                 Former college instructor

"It's refreshing to see a positive curriculum that provides real answers for today's teens. I give it an A+."
                                 Community college student, age eighteen

"I thought it was an awesome, awesome curriculum. It was a good message, especially for teens like me who don't know how important purity is. It should be spread throughout the nation."

High-school student, age fifteen

"Before going to *The True Love Thing to Do* seminar, I had already had a belief in abstinence. After going to the seminar, my beliefs were reinforced and I had a better background to share my beliefs with my peers. It was very enjoyable, with its discussion-type format. I was given many facts about abstinence."

University student, age eighteen

"What I liked about this booklet is that it scientifically and logically explains how free sex is socially damaging and how it shatters that old idea 'Do what you feel, and if it's not hurting anyone else, it's okay.' I also liked how this booklet empowers young adults, teenagers, and pre-teens who are planning to stay virgins until they marry. I think this idea should be taught in public and private schools."

High-school student, age seventeen

"I think the program is very helpful, and has given me a new perspective on dating, abstinence, and marriage."

High-school student, age fifteen

THE TRUE LOVE
THING TO DO

Also by Peter Falkenberg Brown

Works in Progress (as of 2019):

Do You Want To Be Free?
Essays on Freedom as the Foundation
of a World of Love and Beauty

The Living Compass of Kindness
and Compassionate Love:
Essays, Poems, and Stories
about Love, Beauty,
and the Mystical Path

Waking Up Dead and Confused Is a
Terrible Thing: Stories about Love,
Life, Death, and Adventure

Striving for Parental Love:
A Practical Guide on Giving
Parental Love to Children
            (out of print)

Visit the author's website at
peterfalkenbergbrown.com
to read essays, stories, and poetry,
and view video talks at
"The Love, Freedom, & the World
Video Channel"

THE TRUE LOVE
THING TO DO

An Interactive Workbook
on Finding Love and
Preparing for an Enduring Marriage

Third Edition

Peter Falkenberg Brown

The World Community Press
Gray, Maine

The World Community Press
Gray, Maine / USA
https://worldcommunitypress.com

© 2000, 2004, 2019 by Peter Falkenberg Brown
All rights reserved. First edition 2000. Second edition 2004.
Third edition 2019

First Edition published as *Abstinence Because of Love.*

Second Edition published as:
The True Love Thing to Do Seminar Workbook:
A Marriage Preparation, Abstinence, & Character Education Seminar
(With some minor, initial iterations of the second edition.)

No part of this book may be reproduced in any form or by any means
without permission in writing from the publisher, except for the inclusion of
brief quotations in a review or essay.

This book takes advantage of modern, digital, print-on-demand technologies
and may, over time, be printed by more than one printer. If you receive a
copy that fails to meet our high expectations of quality, please inform us by
emailing:

publishers@worldcommunitypress.com

Visit this Web address for more information:

https://worldcommunitypress.com/tl

Cover and interior design by The World Community Press.
~ A swan was used because swans mate for life and are monogamous.

Cover Photo: Reflection of white swan on a misty calm pond.
© Hannu Viitanen | Dreamstime.com

Back cover photo of author by James Chantler Brown
Photo of Hummingbird in Logo by Richard Rodvold

ISBN: 978-0-9635706-2-8

Edition date: October 28, 2019

I dedicate this book to the millions of teenagers and young adults who are searching for love, and happy and fulfilling relationships.

Love may seem to be an unattainable goal or a corny ideal for some, but it is not. Love is within everyone's reach, especially if we approach the search for love with the right emotional and intellectual tools. Love does not have to be "the luck of the draw."

Love is generated from within each of us. As we become "Beings of Love," our environment and atmosphere change, creating a magnetic resonance with other loving individuals.

This volume is offered to all of you who are willing to consider the idea that "love begets love."

Contents

Part One

SESSION ONE

(20 minutes of Reading / 10 minutes of Discussion)

SESSION TWO

(20 minutes of Reading / 10 minutes of Discussion)

~ 10-Minute Break ~

Part Two

SESSION THREE

(25 minutes of Reading / 10 minutes of Discussion)

SESSION FOUR

(15 minutes of Reading / 10 minutes of Discussion)

~ 10-Minute Break ~

Part Three

SESSION FIVE

(30 minutes of Reading / 10 minutes of Discussion)

Contents

❧

How to Read This Book

This book can be read alone, or in a group discussion format. It was originally written as a small book, then restructured as a seminar workbook, and has finally evolved into a book that can also be used as a seminar workbook.

If you read it by yourself, you may wish to approach it as a "seminar for one" and spend time studying the discussion questions and "Quotes to Live By."

If you read it with one friend, or in a small group of friends, or as part of a formal seminar, the "roundtable" format provides a starting point for discussion. After a seminar, the book also serves as a handy source of what may prove to be inspirational and helpful content.

The font size of the text is larger than usual, to promote ease of reading in front of a group.

From the Text . . .

As teenagers approach the
realm of love and romance,
they need to ask themselves
about their long-term goals.

Do they want to reach the age
of eighty, having had multiple
marriages and numerous
affairs, with emotional
wreckage and disillusionment
littering the landscape behind
them, or do they want to go
through life holding hands
with their one true love?

Preface

This book was originally published in 2000 as a small volume titled *Abstinence Because of Love*. In 2004 it evolved into a seminar workbook titled *The True Love Thing to Do Seminar Workbook: A Marriage Preparation, Abstinence, and Character Education Seminar*. Seminars were conducted with that workbook with excellent feedback from sponsors and participants.

I've now decided to release a newly revised and expanded version as a hybrid of the two: a conveniently sized book that still contains the workbook elements of discussion questions, centered on a roundtable format. The new name, *The True Love Thing to Do: An Interactive Workbook on Finding Love and Preparing for an Enduring Marriage*, reflects the new format.

Many abstinence education programs provide important information about AIDS and sexually transmitted diseases, but this book seeks to fill a niche in its coverage of the healthy maturation and maintenance of love as a primary motivator for young people to remain abstinent until marriage, and then remain faithful within marriage.

Because the book deals with the ethics of unselfish love and unselfish human relationships, I believe that the curriculum will help provide young people with direction for the growth of their character. It will help them manage their everyday relationships in an unselfish and ethical manner, and will positively influence the issues of conflict resolution, responsibility, and honesty in the home, in schools, and in the workplace. Encouraging young people to adopt "The True Love Thing to Do" as an ethical viewpoint of unselfish love and service will also be of great benefit to employers in small businesses, larger corporations, and organizations.

My hope is that young people will gain a new vision and understanding of marriage that is centered upon unselfish love, and will thus gain the hope and emotional power to maintain their purity and prepare themselves for marriage, parenting, and an unselfish life that will contribute to a world of peace.

The book has been designed for seminars that can be hosted by anyone, with groups of any size, in any venue. No training is required. A seminar is easy to produce, because it uses a "Reading / Discussion" format that is driven by the participants. A seminar can be as simple as two people reading and discussing the book together, and in fact can be read and reflected upon as a "seminar for one."

The True Love Thing to Do is available for bulk purchases for use in churches or schools, etc, or as wholesale purchases for resellers, both at a substantial discount. Note that copying is not allowed and is an infringement of copyright law. Contact the publisher at the web address or email below for information about bulk or wholesale purchases.

http://worldcommunitypress.com/tl

publishers@worldcommunitypress.com

In spite of the complexities of today's world, with its enormous differences of viewpoint about almost everything, I have personally found that life does indeed have signposts that can guide us through the maze of life's decisions.

I believe in the simplicity of love: the love that cares for others' feelings; the love that inspires joy and beauty; the love that is kind and compassionate toward all.

That love creates strength and resolve to treat others well and to do the right thing—the true love thing—when presented with difficult choices.

Peter Falkenberg Brown
Gray, Maine

Acknowledgments

I could not have written this book without the help of the many family members, friends, and teachers who have encouraged my writing over the years. The "believing eyes" of others is a great and wonderful gift.

I also thank Renee "Eagle Eye" Corley for her excellent copyediting skills.

I most certainly could not have written this book without the kind and compassionate love of God that touches all of us. Thus, as a writer, I can most gratefully say:

> *Deus est auctor amoris et decoris.*
> (God is the author of love and beauty.)

A Note about the Language, Vocabulary, and Examples Used in This Book

This book was written for teenagers and young people in their twenties. The text was specifically written in a non-religious fashion with the goal of being relevant to individuals of any background, religious or otherwise. The text is based on the simple, universal premise that love is appealing to everyone.

My goal is to publish the book in multiple languages, including but not limited to Spanish, Russian, French, Chinese, and Japanese. (If you're interested in translating it, please contact the publishers.)

Because of the difficulties in translating idiomatic English or the current brand of teenage slang, I have decided to stay away from using phrases that might be difficult to translate. Instead, I've written the text in

Standard English with the intention of making the meaning as clear as possible.

Some of the words might be a bit tough for a thirteen-year-old—but should prove easy enough for older teenagers. Even thirteen-year-olds may have read books such as *The Wind in the Willows* or *Tom Sawyer*, which include phrases such as:

> . . . the brutal minions of the law fell upon the hapless Toad . . .

> . . . when he [Tom] climbed cautiously in at the window, he uncovered an ambuscade, in the person of his aunt; and when she saw the state his clothes were in, her resolution to turn his Saturday holiday into captivity at hard labor became adamantine in its firmness.

I promise that I won't use the words "ambuscade" or "adamantine" anywhere in the book. However, I will use the word "minion." ☺

I've also included glossaries of definitions at the end of some of the sections that contain words that may require more explanation. The examples in the text are written for clarity of meaning and for multiple cultures. The reader has full license to adjust the text to fit his or her local culture. How do you say, "Radical, dude!" in Chinese?

On a textual note, grammatical purists may note that I use the "singular their." Since the dictionary lists a usage of "their" as "used after an indefinite singular antecedent in place of the definite masculine form 'his' or the definite feminine form 'her,'" I'm fine with the "singular their."

I have also decided "to boldly go" into the frontier of split infinitives, and place adverbs inside some verb phrases, perhaps because I like Star Trek and perhaps because doing so is not as taboo as it once was.

Readers may notice that the font size is slightly larger than usual. It has been designed that way to facilitate easy reading when standing in front of a group.

~ minion: *n.* An obsequious follower or dependent; a sycophant.

~ ambuscade: *n.* An ambush.

~ adamantine: *adj.* Unyielding; inflexible.

Note to Seminar Moderators:
Recommended Seminar Format

Schedule

(See the Table of Contents for a schedule breakdown.)

The True Love Thing to Do seminar has been created to follow a "Reading / Discussion" format. Students follow the text in their workbooks while one or more readers in the front of the room reads the text. It takes an average of about one and a half minutes to read one full page.

The seminar is broken into three parts, with a ten-minute refreshment break in between each part. It's also possible to host the seminar on different days, divided into parts. Each section consists of readings and roundtable discussions. The seminar takes approximately three hours in total.

Seminar Moderator

The entire seminar may be staffed by one person, who serves as a moderator. The function of the moderator is minimal but important. The more that the participants do, the better. The moderator's main jobs are to keep things moving on time, to answer questions that arise, to help select readers, discussion moderators, and table reporters, and to generally ensure that things go smoothly.

Readers

Although it's possible to conduct the seminar with one reader for all five sessions, it provides variety if each session—or at least each part—has a different reader.

The quality of the reading is critical to the success of the seminar, so readers should read at the right pace (not too quickly!) and should enunciate. Thus, the moderator should choose the readers with care. Note that the Discussion Questions can also be read by the reader, to prepare the students for the roundtable discussions.

Roundtable Discussions

After the text and questions are read, the students participate in roundtable discussions. The essential point is that the students talk over the discussion topics in small groups, even if the tables are rectangular or even if you have no tables at all. The roundtable discussion topics are meant as guidelines and can certainly be modified by an experienced moderator.

Depending upon the length of the seminar, it may not be possible for each group to cover all of the topics listed. At the discretion of the seminar leader, each group may pick the topics that they want to discuss. It's not necessary to cover all the topics—the main point is that the students engage in a lively discussion. Ten minutes is a good time frame for a discussion, in order to limit the total seminar time to three hours.

The moderator should issue a one-minute warning toward the end of each discussion. It may be appropriate, depending upon the age of the students or the opinion of the seminar leader, to divide the roundtable discussion groups by gender. However, the seminar does not cover anything explicit, and thus should not ordinarily cause embarrassment.

Discussion Moderators

Each table or group should have a discussion leader or moderator who will make every effort to keep the discussion on track and moving forward. It's important that each student has a chance to voice his or her own opinions; thus the table moderator needs to guide people to not talk too long and to be considerate of others' opinions.

If there are no discussion leaders on staff, then the group can choose a discussion leader from the participants seated at the table. In fact, the students are usually pleased to be selected as discussion leaders and reporters.

Table Reporters

Each table should have a student notetaker, who writes down brief bullets or prose about each person's comments. The table reporter may then be called upon by the seminar leader to report to the entire group about the conclusions or views that were expressed at the table. Note that not every table needs to report; it's entirely dependent upon time. The reports should be brief, usually one or two minutes, and the reporter should read the questions that the comments covered.

Online Links:

Online Evaluation Form

A link to an online evaluation form is included at the back of the workbook. Moderators and participants can fill out the evaluation form, if they wish, to provide feedback and suggestions about the workbook, as well as to provide any comments or quotes about the text and the seminar experience.

Graduation Certificate

A link to a Graduation Certificate is also included at the back of the book. Moderators are encouraged to print the certificate and present it to each student after graduation.

Telling Others about the Book and Seminar

You are invited to tell others about the book and seminar. In fact, you can make a very substantial commission on sales of the book to groups. See the link at the back of the book for more information.

Booking the Author as a Public Speaker

Peter Falkenberg Brown is available for public speaking bookings. For more information, see the Online Links section at the back of the book.

SESSION ONE

The True Love Thing to Do

Sexual Activity
and the Realm of Heart, Part 1

Roundtable Discussions

Quotes to Live By

The True Love Thing to Do

*W*hy should we save ourselves till marriage, and why is this "the true love thing to do"? When we fall madly in love with someone at the ripe old age of fifteen, sixteen, or even younger, we don't want to think about anything except our newfound love. Why should we refrain from having sex with our new girl-friend or boyfriend? Why should we prepare ourselves for marriage, and how can we do that?

There are thousands of messages blaring at us to convince us that "if it feels good, do it," or "the animals do it, so why shouldn't we?" Sex is everywhere, and living together without marriage has become more and more popular. There are so many divorces, and so many teenagers who have seen how difficult marriage can be, that the ancient concepts of true love, courtship, and faithful marriage are in severe danger of disappearing altogether. Some teenagers might even say, "We enjoy

3

sex. Why should we stop having sex, and why should we wait until marriage when we don't even believe in marriage?"

Hard questions indeed. Sex does feel good, most especially when love is present. We hope to answer these questions more, in the course of this seminar. Our hope is that by the end of this seminar (even though we all might not agree with everything), we all can still say: "Preparing for marriage is a topic worth talking about." Examining life with an active mind and talking about things that matter will open up new options for our future. When it comes to sex and love, we all want the brightest future possible.

This seminar doesn't push old-fashioned traditions, the status quo, or the newest thing. Human beings owe it to themselves to lead an examined life. It doesn't make sense to agree with something just because "everyone's doing it" or because "it's always been that way." Consider women's rights. For thousands of years, women couldn't vote and had no rights. (This is still the case in some countries today.) Because the repression of women was a time-honored tradition, was it right? Of course not.

Teenagers, who are vastly more intelligent than they're sometimes given credit for, need the information that will allow them to make decisions about life based on common sense, logic, and deep reflection about the right questions.

This seminar breaks with some popular opinions by taking the approach that we should postpone sexual activity until marriage not just because of safe sex, pregnancies, or other external factors, but because of love itself. True love to be exact. The term "true love" has fallen into disrepute, perhaps because of the gigantic failure rate in relationships but also certainly because of the cynicism in our culture today. We need to take a moment to look at the term "true love" and see if we can actually use it and appreciate it as a valid goal to strive for in our lives.

Before we look at the question, "Why is preparing ourselves for marriage the true love thing to do?" we need to establish a foundation for our discussion. For example, if we were only machines, without feelings, it wouldn't make sense to discuss true love. It wouldn't have any meaning for us. Luckily for us, we're more than machines. We're living, breathing people who all share certain common traits that allow us to communicate about mutual ideas, hopes, and dreams. The desire for love is a human characteristic that cuts across all boundary lines such as race, language, or culture.

Even though various cultures in history have created many different outlooks about love, it should be possible to peel away the layers of tradition and arrive at a philosophical viewpoint about love that makes sense to most of us. To do that, we start this seminar by examining basic concepts about love.

It's not good enough to be simplistic in our definition of true love. It's important to understand true love with our heart, not just our mind—and to feel it through our experience. Therefore, let's explore that vast uncharted area called our heart, by looking at our own life experience.

❧   ❧   ❧

If we think back to our earliest memory, what comes to our mind? No matter how old or sophisticated we might have become, for many of us it's usually the memory of our father and mother caring for us. Perhaps we remember their kind faces peering down at us as we awoke from a comfortable nap. We may remember them feeding us or playing with us with our favorite toy.

Our memories of our very early childhood are often precious, because they are frequently memories of being loved unconditionally by one or both of our parents, or perhaps by our grandparents.

As we grew older, our relationship with our parents may have grown more complex—especially when we became teenagers. Life is often confusing, and sometimes we might have lost sight of the fact that our parents have loved us many, many times in our life. If we feel hurt by our parents, it's still very important to remember the love that they *did* express.

It's rather like the scales of justice. Did they give us more love than experiences of pain, or the other way around? Did they sincerely try to love us? Was their intent good? It's not always easy to be fair to our parents, but it's important to try, not just for their sake but also for our own. The more we recognize and value their love for us, the happier we will be, because knowing that we are loved, and feeling the love that flows to us, brings us joy.

The love that many of us received and felt as young children, coming from our parents, is called parental love. It was special because it was unselfish love. Sometimes we might have taken it for granted, or not really thought about it at all. It isn't easy to understand parental love if we don't yet have children, or at least have spent a lot of time with children. Parental love is related very closely with true love, so let's examine parental love a bit more.

Think of a very young child whom you know— perhaps a brother or sister, or a cousin or family friend. When you look at a three-year-old and see how cute they can be, and see how much they love to smile and play, don't you feel delighted inside? Doesn't that particular little boy or girl make you smile and make you want to give them a gift, or something especially yummy to eat?

If you smiled just now, or even thought about smiling, it means that you are already experiencing unselfish love!

7

You are on the way to becoming a person of parental love—someone who cares for the happiness of others.

Of course, parental love is more than smiling at a cute little boy or girl. Parental love is deep and profound and patient. Parental love is willing to endure yucky diapers and temper tantrums and other uncomfortable things. Parental love can even see past awful monstrosities like pimples on the end of one's nose. Didn't your mother comfort you when you were staring at the mirror in agony?

What is the highest form of love? If we use the yardsticks of unselfishness and kindness and compassion, we would have to say that *genuine* parental love is the most unselfish. One way of describing parental love is to say that a person of parental love will look at another person and say, "I want to bring true happiness to this person. I want to care for this person in such a way that I can influence his happiness for the rest of his life."

Let's not confuse the virtue of parental love with the fact that parents are sometimes immature and may not resonate very much at all with parental love. The selfish actions of unloving parents do *not* invalidate the beauty of kind and compassionate parental love. Thus, even though the reality of parents is that they often have to work very hard to actually *be parental* in their quality of love, parental love itself is a wonderful and valuable attribute of human life.

A parental person will want to serve the other person, give to the other person, and love the other person. A crucial aspect of parental love is that the parental person will think about the other person's happiness in long-range terms. If we love someone unselfishly, we want him or her to be happy forever, don't we?

At the same time, a parental person will be thoughtful, reflecting deeply about the real way that the other person can find true happiness. For example, when, as children, we wanted to do something that was not good for us (such as eating ten candy bars in a row) our parents hopefully stopped us—because they knew we would suffer later if we ate them.

We, as shortsighted children, may not have understood our parents—we might have kicked and screamed in rebellion. Our parents, on the other hand, were thinking about our long-term happiness and usually were motivated by an unselfish desire to care for us.

Once in a while we might have felt that our parents fell short of the standard of true love. Honest parents will be the first to admit that *everyone* falls short of the highest standard of parental and unselfish love. Yet, our parents try hard, so the most loving thing for us to do, as children, is to support them, love them, and do our best to help them build relationships of harmony and love. (After all, if we're so much better than our parents, why aren't we loving them more than they're loving us?)

Examining ourselves tends to help us become more humble.

When we remember the parental love that we received, it helps us recognize true love now, both in ourselves and in others. We need to maintain or fix what I call our "emotional radar" or "the radar of heart." We all have a special radar system. Our emotional radar is invisible and is used to sense and perceive the invisible feelings flowing between our heart and the hearts of others. We all have this capability. Think of the time that you walked into a room and could feel that the atmosphere between the people in the room was cold and brittle because of an argument between them.

Unfortunately, our emotional radar gets rusty because we don't use it enough in our fast-paced culture. Sometimes it might have become damaged because we didn't have the opportunity to adequately experience love in our family relationships.

Our radar of heart is profoundly important, because our ability to understand the feelings and the concepts of true love, or unselfish and parental love, will directly impact our relationships with the opposite sex. The term "true love," in this context, means unselfish love, which contains within it the heart of parental love toward others, even if the other person is not our child. One can be, and should be, kind, compassionate, and parental toward everyone, even one's husband or wife.

Using the term "true love" shouldn't feel shallow or embarrassing, because it contains within it the virtues of kindness, compassion, patience, and profound respect for the other person as a unique human being. It is, in essence, the motivational core of the Golden Rule: to treat others with love as we wish to be loved ourselves. In fact, the terms "true love," "parental love," and "unselfish love" could just as easily be replaced with "kind and compassionate love."

Just to be clear: when we feel compassionate or "parental" love toward our husband or wife it does *not* mean that we are their parent and they are our child. (Parents don't marry their children.) It's just one way to describe the *depth* of compassionate love.

If we think about true love in this in-depth way, it becomes a very real, very practical term for the kind of relationship of heart that we all want to have.

With this exploration of our heart as the foundation of our discussion, we can say that true love is more than an incidental part of sexual activity. True love is the core guidepost for sexual activity, and the main reason that we should save ourselves, and prepare ourselves, for marriage.

~ disrepute: *n.* Damage to or loss of reputation.

~ status quo: *n.* The existing condition or state of affairs.

Sexual Activity
and the Realm of Heart, Part 1

It is possible for someone to engage in sexual activity with many, many different partners. Some might say that living one's life in this way is not wrong—that it is our right to do as we wish with our physical body—and that if we seek sexual pleasure with multiple partners, it is our own affair, since it "doesn't hurt anybody."

We hear about the hang-ups of the Victorians and the sexual ignorance of past generations, and may feel grateful that we live in an enlightened age in which sexuality is seen as a healthy part of the human experience. And indeed that is correct: Sexuality is meant to be a healthy part of our lives. This leads to the question: "What is healthy sexuality?"

Since most forms of sexuality are not illegal, and since sexuality is generally private, it is common now (for

Westerners, at least) to have the attitude that one's sexual activities are nobody else's business. It is also a common view that it's important to test the waters and see if one is sexually compatible with a potential love interest, so it seems normal to many to have sex before marriage.

The True Love Thing to Do is not based on Victorian prudery or outdated laws about sexuality. Individual rights are important, and couples should strive to have healthy sexual relationships. To support the goal of healthy sexual relationships, the central theme of *The True Love Thing to Do* is *love*. Love contains many attributes, but one of the most important is that our "love" does not cause harm to the other person—or to ourselves.

Let's go back to the idea that if we seek sexual pleasure with a partner—or multiple partners over a period of time—it is our own affair, since it "doesn't hurt anybody." Let's put that idea to the test.

Do No Harm

Human behavior is usually not black or white, but is instead influenced by a complex set of motivations. There are many gray areas in our thought patterns and desires that often go unnoticed.

When two people fall in love, it seems normal nowadays to kiss and then make love. The falling in love part of that scenario isn't even a prerequisite. Just feeling attracted to each other is often quite enough. One might ask, "Well, what's wrong with that?"

At first glance it may seem perfectly fine to have sex whenever and wherever one wants to, because doing so fits quite well into the current cultural paradigm of "what's cool." Who wants to be uncool? Being cool may seem to be incredibly important, but what if we found out that having casual sex harmed others?

Let's step back for a moment and look at the types of relationships between young men and women. A sample list for today's culture might include:

- casual friends, with no sex
- good friends, with no sex

- friends "with benefits," i.e., sex
- flings and one-night stands
- ongoing, casual sexual relationships
- first dates, with or without sex
- ongoing dates, with or without sex
- girlfriend and boyfriend, with or without sex
- engaged couples, with or without sex
- committed long-term relationships with sex, but without marriage
- married couples

Putting aside the relationships of "friends, with no sex," let's look at the relationships that include either romance or sex, or both. What sets them apart from relationships as friends is *intimacy*.

Romance and sex happen at a deeper level of intimacy than one experiences with friends. Casual sex with no emotional commitment still requires physical intimacy that goes far beyond platonic relationships. When emotions are involved, from either person, then sexual, physical intimacy is deepened by emotional intimacy.

Is it not true that the common thread that runs through most romantic and sexual relationships is a desire to be loved? I say "most," because some individuals embark on sexual relationships with little or no regard for the feelings of the other persons. Some young men and women may callously ignore the feelings of their conquests and care very little if they leave emotional damage behind. At their worst, these encounters devolve into the crimes of rape or sexual abuse. In other cases, two people may meet and embark on a sexual relationship with equal disregard for the other's feelings (such as the relationships between prostitutes and their customers).

Although generalizing is not always accurate, isn't it a reasonable statement to say that romantic and sexual relationships usually include a very strong desire for love in the heart of at least *one* of the participants?

That desire for love provides the key motivating factor to examine romance and sex more deeply. From dating all the way to marriage, the individuals involved want to be loved (at some level) and hopefully want to also *give love* to their partners.

Many individuals have not been raised, trained, or educated very well to focus their mind and heart on the extraordinary and wonderful practice of loving other people. It is a practice that is frequently and woefully absent from homes, schools, and our society at large. It is true that many societies include standards of courtesy, politeness, etiquette, charity, and "being nice" to others. Yet, how often do we hear of the idea that it's a very good thing to wake up in the morning with the goal that "today I will love people"?

The True Love Thing to Do at its core is about caring for other people with kindness, compassion, and *love*. Looking at others and digging into how they're feeling, and considering if and how our actions or words are making them feel better or worse, are central elements of loving other people. When that other person is our romantic and/or sexual partner, then an important question is, "Am I bringing them joy or bringing them sadness and harm?"

I think most people don't set out to hurt others as they develop romantic or sexual relationships. It is, however, a sad reality that it is often just one person who breaks off the relationship, thus causing pain to the other. Some pain is unavoidable, since it's hard to know if a relationship will work until time has passed. Therefore, as people explore new relationships and look for "the one," it's important to find ways to minimize any potential harm to the other person.

Some people don't care about the harm they cause others. We might imagine a man like that—let's call him "Apollo Stone." He sits in his home, feet on the kitchen table, singing an old Elvin Bishop song:

> I must have been through about a million girls
> I'd love 'em then I'd leave 'em alone
> I didn't care how much they cried, no sir
> Their tears left me cold as a stone

Who wants to be like him? Or the feminine version, "Aphrodite Grim," clicking down the steps with her stiletto heels, searching for disposable men?

No, we don't want to be like them, but instead hope that we can find our one true love without leaving broken hearts behind us on the way.

We also don't want to damage *our own heart*, which is a strong possibility unless we're careful. We can be damaged because of heartbreak, which is strong and palpable. But we can also damage our soul and emotions gradually, as we go from one relationship to another, digging deeper and deeper ruts of disappointment and cynicism.

Wouldn't it be better to manage our relationships so that we can preserve a fresh and hopeful heart? It is entirely possible.

From the Text . . .

Teenagers, who are vastly more intelligent than they're sometimes given credit for, need the information that will allow them to make decisions about life based on common sense, logic, and deep reflection about the right questions.

Session One
Roundtable Discussion Topics

1. What is true love, and why is it important?

2. Is it possible for everyone to experience true love? What are some of the ways that parents express true love to their children?

3. What are some of the ways that we can express love unselfishly?

4. What is our "emotional radar"? Why does our radar become "rusty" and insensitive in our relationships to others? How can we keep our radar in good repair, so that we can easily sense and understand the feelings of others?

5. Is it true that human beings find the most happiness in giving love to others and receiving love in return? Is love the thing that we like the most?

6. Is it true that hurting others and causing others pain is something to be avoided whenever possible? Do we feel happy or sad when we hurt someone?

7. Is it a good thing to wake up in the morning with the goal that "today I will love people"?

Quotes to Live By
from Session One

☙ "Preparing for marriage is a topic worth talking about." Examining life with an active mind and talking about things that matter will open up new options for our future. When it comes to sex and love, we all want the brightest future possible.

☙ This seminar doesn't push old-fashioned traditions, the status quo, or the newest thing. Human beings owe it to themselves to lead an examined life. It doesn't make sense to agree with something just because "everyone's doing it" or because "it's always been that way."

☙ If we love someone unselfishly, we want him or her to be happy forever, don't we?

❧ Our emotional radar is invisible, and is used to sense and perceive the invisible feelings flowing between our heart and the hearts of others.

❧ One can be, and should be, kind, compassionate, and parental toward everyone, even one's husband or wife.

❧ True love is the core guidepost for sexual activity, and the main reason that we should save ourselves, and prepare ourselves, for marriage.

❧ How often do we hear of the idea that it's a very good thing to wake up in the morning with the goal that "today, I will love people"?

SESSION TWO

Sexual Activity
and the Realm of Heart, Part 2

Sex Should Be Unselfish

Roundtable Discussions

Quotes to Live By

10-Minute Break

Sexual Activity
and the Realm of Heart, Part 2

*W*hen we imagine the exaggerated characters of Apollo Stone or Aphrodite Grim, we highlight one of the great dilemmas of life. As individuals, we constantly search for happiness and fulfillment. Yet often, in our search, we find that we have hurt others, even though we didn't plan to hurt them. When it's pointed out to us that we have hurt someone, we usually feel sorry. Very few people will stand up in the middle of the local shopping mall and yell out that they're really proud of themselves because they hurt a lot of people that day.

When we look at history, we see that tyrants or criminals are reviled because they brought suffering to others. Prisons, in fact, are mostly occupied by people who hurt others through selfish and unloving actions. Unselfishness is—to some degree or another—the accepted standard or goal in society. How many of us look toward the rest of our life, saying, "I hope that I can hurt hundreds of people before I die"?

We bring others joy or pain through our interaction with them. Whether in conversation or our actions, we are in the position where we inadvertently may hurt someone. If we ask ourselves, "Do we feel happy when we hurt someone?" the answer will probably be "no." Even though a selfish man might not care about people very much, he usually would be reluctant to say that he felt pleasure at the suffering of others, if only to appear normal to others.

Sometimes for the sake of pride (but more often because we believe it to be so), most of us would agree that the right standard is that we shouldn't cause others pain. Conversely, we feel quite proud of ourselves if someone comes up to us and says, "You know, you really made me happy!"

What is the essence of this nature in people that yearns for joy and happiness? When do we feel the most joy? Although money, power, and knowledge are high on the list of things that people desire, isn't it true that love is the thing that makes us happiest?

When our fictional Apollo Stone withdrew his love from the many different women that he romanced, they might have cried. One or more might have cried for days.

Isn't it true that the removal of love causes people great pain?

But wait, you say . . . Apollo didn't set out to love all of those women. He just wanted to have sex with them. He was seeking his own physical pleasure. He didn't remove his love—he didn't have any love to begin with. You are right, of course. His desires were self-centered. He didn't think about the happiness of those women. It wasn't important to him.

Let's think for a moment, though. Unless both partners engaged in sex are 100 percent cold-hearted and self-centered, one of them is going to get hurt when the relationship of love deteriorates. Since no one is really a machine, we can conclude that everyone gets hurt, even if they don't acknowledge or recognize their own pain.

The very nature of sex tends to include the aspect of love, of romance, and of heart. How many people do you know who habitually have sex together with absolutely no regard for each other? Certainly we don't want to be like that ourselves.

It is safe to say, then, that the normal standard of behavior and heart that most of us will agree with is the standard that says, "I don't want to hurt anyone. I don't want to cause anyone any grief. Rather, I hope that I can bring joy to others by caring for them, serving them, and loving them as much as possible."

People, ourselves included, receive joy when they are cared for and loved. No one wants to be cruelly mistreated. For our part, isn't it true that we feel very, very conscience-stricken when we find that we have hurt someone? We are anxious to rectify the wrong that we have done, and restore the person's feelings.

Our basic heart, then, as a person, is that we feel the most joy when we care for others and are loved in return. Kindness and compassionate love toward others are virtues on the measuring stick of goodness that is common to all of us. We all admire unselfish people.

Is sexual activity any different? Of course not!

Sexual activity, more than any other human activity, is linked to the realm of emotions by its very nature. Even those persons who engage in casual sexual activity will admit that they want to be loved by their sexual partner. They certainly don't want to be hated or abused by their partner!

~ rectify: *tr.v.* To set right; correct.

Sex Should Be Unselfish

If our primary ethic in life is to treat others unselfishly, and to serve and give and love with kindness and compassion, then with what attitude should we approach the activity of sex? If the thought of causing others suffering makes us feel sad, then it stands to reason that we would not want to hurt anyone because of our sexual activity.

Our desire to love others with an unselfish and kind heart becomes the guidepost for our sexual activity. As in all other aspects of our life, our desire to make others happy will lead us to act unselfishly in our sexual relationship with our one true love, before and after we're married.

What does this mean, in concrete terms?

An overly ardent young man might say to a young lady, "If you really loved me, you would have sex with me!" (This, of course, before they were married.)

The young lady might be confused. Having feelings of love for the young man, she might oblige him, thinking that she was being unselfish and giving. This happens all the time, doesn't it?

However, the standard of unselfish love should cause the young woman to step back and say, "Wait. . . . What is best for our relationship of love from a long-term point of view? What will cause our love to flourish and become unselfish and permanent? What will create a relationship of true love?"

An easier way to understand this is to look at it from the young man's point of view. As you may have heard, young men have strong and sometimes overwhelming sexual desires.

Young men tend to feel sexual desire toward many different women, often quite indiscriminately. How many times have young men looked at young women and felt sexual desire that had nothing to do with unselfish love?

When a young man feels sexual desire for a young woman, how will he answer if he is asked, "At this moment of sexual desire, are you thinking of the young woman's lifelong happiness? Are you thinking of bringing her true joy? Are you thinking of caring for her for many years to come, even when she is old and wrinkled? Or are you just thinking of her physical body, and your own sexual stimulation?"

These are very difficult and uncomfortable questions. They are also the kind of questions that are tremendously illuminating and useful. It is helpful to remind ourselves—whether we are young men or young women—that we really do want to become unselfish and loving people. Don't we?

Because of our own desire to become better, it is liberating (although initially confronting) to ask ourselves these hard questions. When we do, we hopefully will be able to tell ourselves, "Well, even though my sexual attitude toward the other person was self-centered, I recognize that now and I want to change and treat the other person unselfishly. I really do want to love the other person with true love."

Adopting an attitude of unselfish love toward the other person will enable us to ask ourselves, "What is best for this person? Is it better to have sex now, when our relationship is still immature and our future together is not guaranteed, or is it better to wait until marriage, when we both have clarified and cemented our mutual commitment of love?"

The crux of the matter is our own spiritual and emotional status. How mature are our mind and our heart when we look at someone of the opposite sex? Does the struggling sixteen-year-old boy (or forty-year-old man, for that matter) really love each woman with a pure heart of unselfish love?

To do so requires that a man looks at only one woman as his wife and all other women as his sisters, cousins, aunts, or grandmothers. If his love is pure and mature, a young married man will look at other beautiful women as his sisters—not as objects to lust after or drool over.

Yet, how often do both men and women fall short of this pure standard of unselfish love? Even one of our presidents was laughed at for his honesty when he admitted that he had committed adultery in his heart. We won't even include the presidents who did more than think about other women. We're not, however, throwing stones at other people's weaknesses. The real issue is that each one of us struggles to love members of the opposite sex in a pure and unselfish way. One might think that looking and thinking are far removed from immoral actions—but they're really not. In this context, the verse, "... every one who looks at a woman lustfully has already committed adultery with her in his heart" (Matthew 5:28, Revised Standard Version) becomes extremely relevant to teenagers.

Spiritual, or internal, emotional love springing from the heart is centered on unselfish caring and affection. Spiritual love must lead and dominate physical, sexual attraction, because the nature of true love is that it cares for the other person forever, no matter how beautiful or ugly the person may be.

Having sex before our spiritual love is mature, outside of a committed marriage, impedes the growth of our unselfish heart of love. This is true because the attraction of sexual love is so strong that it can easily dominate and confuse immature, spiritual love. It's very damaging to teenagers' hearts to have sex before their love is mature.

It's also true that people get married when they're eighteen or twenty, and at that time their hearts are not yet mature. There's one big difference: Because they're married and (hopefully) committed to each other, their hearts can grow together in love and they can protect each other. Without that rock-solid commitment of marriage, one's heart can become bruised and battered like a wood chip on the ocean.

The proper growth of our unselfish heart of love may not seem like a very urgent matter to us, especially when we feel like we're "in love," but it directly impacts our ability to give true love to the person we think we love. Being "abstinent because of love" means that we're abstinent for the sake of the other person's heart as well as our own.

We want to protect the other person's feelings, protect their life from troubles and difficulties, and protect them from damage in any way. Young men of true love will want to help the young lady they admire become a better and more mature person.

Sex is, and should be, the most intimate and holy part of a committed, long-term relationship of love. Knowing that, a young man of true love will say, "Let's save that most precious part of our love until we're committed to each other in marriage."

As teenagers approach the realm of love and romance, they need to ask themselves about their long-term goals. Do they want to reach the age of eighty, having had multiple marriages and numerous affairs, with emotional wreckage and disillusionment littering the landscape behind them, or do they want to go through life holding hands with their one true love?

Imagine having just one relationship. The young man and woman marry and dedicate their hearts to each other. They determine to love each other "beyond death"— beyond any problems or struggles or distractions. They devote their energies to caring for each other (as well as others) and to communicating their feelings to each other on a daily basis, sharing their innermost heart and thoughts. As they work hard to care for each other (and it is work, sometimes), their love for each other grows and grows, until their minds and hearts meld into something wonderful and greater than either of them.

When they have sex together, it is a reflection of their true love for each other, and the love they have for the children that may be born from that union. Sex based on true love becomes a holy and spiritual activity, because the motivation for it is "heart"—the unselfish and golden core of each person. Sex based on true love is physically pleasurable—but the heart of love between the husband and wife creates an experience that is far more than physical.

In direct contrast, teenagers who engage in casual sex damage their own heart and the hearts of their partners. Their ability to create a relationship of true love becomes damaged, as their emotional radar becomes rusty and dull. The rich sensitivity of their heart grows dim, and when they do have sex with a partner, it tends to be extremely non-spiritual—relegated to the realm where physical sensations overshadow their spiritual and emotional sensitivities. True love is often completely absent. Even when the partners feel strong emotion for each other, it simply doesn't compare to the closeness that can be attained when one devotes oneself to loving one person forever.

It's hard to discuss things like "eternal true love" without examining deeper issues about the nature of human beings and the *source* of unselfish love. The question of whether or not human beings are simply animals randomly evolved from rocks and dust—or something more—directly affects our attitude toward love.

Harvard Ph.D. Patrick Glynn writes in *God: The Evidence* that scientists are now realizing that the universe was designed from the subatomic level to support the lives of human beings. Even the smallest changes in forces such as gravity would have made human life impossible. The concept of design leads inevitably to the "God or no God" question. Those in favor of the view that everything in the universe was designed by God point to evidence that is becoming increasingly difficult to dispute.

Is it realistic to think that the presidents' faces on Mount Rushmore evolved randomly, without human intervention? Could the rain and wind have reproduced their faces so exactly? In the same way, it's more logical to assume that the powerful yet invisible force called love has its source in a living Creator, rather than evolving from clouds of minerals and particles. The entire family system, with fathers and mothers and children, and all the potential for love contained in family relationships, provide clues to the invisible nature of a compassionate and intelligent source.

One of the most fascinating clues is the human desire for love to last forever. When we feel deep love for someone, we want it to *last*. This seems to indicate that the Creator of our desire for eternal love also wants our relationships of love to last forever. Although studying these questions in depth is beyond the scope of this seminar, the logical conclusion that there is an afterlife or spirit world, where our love for our eternal husband or wife will continue forever, provides immense and even revolutionary meaning to the commitment of marriage.

The view that sex was created by a Universal Intelligence to be part of a loving marriage adds an infinite and spiritual dimension to the sexual relationship and to the realm of heart created between a husband and wife who are committed to love each other forever. A marriage such as this requires effort and time—but the quality of love developed by the husband and wife is better than the love found in any fairy tale.

From the Text . . .

If the thought of causing
others suffering makes us feel
sad, then it stands to reason
that we would not want to
hurt anyone because of our
sexual activity.

From the Text . . .

Our desire to love others with an unselfish and kind heart becomes the guidepost for our sexual activity.

Session Two
Roundtable Discussion Topics

1. If we express love to someone and then drop them and break the relationship, does the other person often feel emotional pain?

2. What can we do to avoid causing pain to the opposite sex?

3. When we do find our "one true love" in the future, how can we build a relationship of true love? What are some steps that we can take to avoid hurting the other person?

4. Should sexual relations always be guided by unselfish love for the other person? Does the other person's future happiness have any relevance in sexual relationships?

5. Is it possible to experience sexual desire for another person without feeling any regard for their personal happiness? Is that a good thing?

6. Why is spiritual and emotional love for the other person more important to a relationship than physical attraction? Does it affect the growth and quality of our spiritual love if we have many sexual encounters before we are fully mature?

7. If we postpone sex until we are married, and then have sex only with our husband or wife, and continually express unselfish love to our spouse, will our sexual and emotional relationship with our spouse be better because we waited? If that is true, why is it true?

Quotes to Live By from Session Two

❧ If we ask ourselves, "Do we feel happy when we hurt someone?" the answer will probably be "no."

❧ Unless both partners engaged in sex are 100 percent cold-hearted and self-centered, one of them is going to get hurt when the relationship of love deteriorates. Since no one is really a machine, we can conclude that everyone gets hurt, even if they don't acknowledge or recognize their own pain.

❧ It is safe to say, then, that the normal standard of behavior and heart that most of us will agree with is the standard that says, "I don't want to hurt anyone. I don't want to cause anyone any grief. Rather, I hope that I can bring joy to others by caring for them, serving them, and loving them as much as possible."

❧ If the thought of causing others suffering makes us feel sad, then it stands to reason that we would not want to hurt anyone because of our sexual activity.

Our desire to love others with an unselfish and kind heart becomes the guidepost for our sexual activity.

❧ Adopting an attitude of unselfish love toward the other person will enable us to ask ourselves, "What is best for this person? Is it better to have sex now, when our relationship is still immature and our future together is not guaranteed, or is it better to wait until marriage, when we both have clarified and cemented our mutual commitment of love?"

❧ Being "abstinent because of love" means that we're abstinent for the sake of the other person's heart as well as our own.

❧ . . . teenagers who engage in casual sex damage their own heart and the hearts of their partners. Their ability to create a relationship of true love becomes damaged, as their emotional radar becomes rusty and dull. The rich sensitivity of their heart grows dim, and when they do have sex with a partner, it tends to be extremely non-spiritual—relegated to the realm where physical sensations overshadow their spiritual and emotional sensitivities.

SESSION THREE

How to Save Ourselves Till Marriage

Roundtable Discussions

Quotes to Live By

How to Save Ourselves Till Marriage

ven when we feel clear inside ourselves that waiting is better, it's still not easy to deal with the constant pressure from others to have sex right away. The message gets blared at us everywhere: from television, from our friends, from the opposite sex (in some cases) and even sometimes from grownups and the latest experts. We get mixed messages, don't we? It's bad enough to get put through the mill of peer pressure. It's even worse when someone in authority tells us that having sex is "natural and inevitable" and thus not worth resisting. Getting handed a condom doesn't really help us to say "no," does it?

To complicate our life even further, sex has become physically dangerous with the threat of AIDS and other sexually transmitted diseases. So-called "safe sex" isn't that safe at all, when one considers the failure rate of condoms. And finally, the message about abstinence has sometimes become a tactic used to confuse already over-stressed teenagers (or their parents). Abstinence has been redefined by some people to mean any type of sexual activity that does not include sexual intercourse. In other words, you can do just about anything short of insertion and supposedly call it "abstinence." That's like saying that you're not really swimming because you didn't get your hair wet.

I think adults should honor and respect teenagers enough to encourage them to meet the highest standards, without muddying the water with psychobabble. The search for legal loopholes (because some people want to have sex and still be able to say that they didn't have sex) has obscured the real issue: how to create marriages and families of true love.

It's time for teenagers to stand up and let people know that they're more than dumb animals run amok. It is possible to save our love for our spouse. Isn't it better to have pride in our inherent capability to be morally strong, intellectually clear, and concerned for the feelings of others? Insisting that sex should be saved for the one we'll love forever is the right thing to do, and the gutsy thing to do. Abstinence, real abstinence, means not having any type of sex. And we're all smart enough, and honest enough, to figure that one out. It isn't, after all, rocket science.

Saving ourselves for marriage and preparing ourselves for marriage are the true love things to do. Anyone who tells us otherwise is inferring that we're not much more than mindless animals. That's not very complimentary, is it?

The best defense against pressure from others to have casual and uncommitted sex is to look them in the eye, with a serious look, and say, "You believe in true, eternal love, don't you?"

Who can say no to that? If they do say no, then you know that they're not the right person for you, anyway.

If they say yes, you've got them. With a generous, magnanimous heart (it's always nice to be magnanimous, isn't it?), firmly remind them that true, eternal love requires, by its definition, a rock-solid, real commitment. Sex is the most intimate part of love, and isn't like a cheap handkerchief to blow one's nose into and casually throw in the trash.

Of course, all the wolves (and maybe even some wolverettes and sirens) out there will say things like, "Oh, but I do love you! That's why we should have sex now!" Look them in the eye and say, "If you really love me eternally, then you will encourage me to save myself until you marry me. If you're not saying that, something's wrong. Period."

Frankly, though, saying no is a really tough thing to do in a society that's pressuring us to have sex now, now,

now. On top of that, we ourselves, as humans, and as teenagers, find it difficult to resist the immediate temptation of sex. That's why the very first line of defense is not at the front door of his or her apartment, after a romantic evening out on the town. Saying no requires that we're clearheaded and strong. Our biggest obstacle is the power of love itself.

Let's be honest. Kissing produces a powerful effect, both for girls and boys. Saying no after a long, romantic kiss is like sampling the buffet when you're starving and then walking out of the restaurant without eating. It just "ain't realistic." So what's the best way to say no and save our love for marriage? Honestly, the best way is to wait to date.

Wait to Date. Courtship 2.0 is Better

No, "wait to date" wasn't a typo. ☺ These days, people start dating, holding hands, and having girlfriends and boyfriends when they're ten, eleven, or twelve years old (or younger). How can we muster up the courage and strength to say no when we're dating all the time?

I know, I know. Now you might be thinking, "Well, how can I meet the person of my dreams, if I don't date?" It's a reasonable question. The answer is really rather simple. We see people all the time—at school, at games and events, and at social functions. At those public events we're safe. Safe, that is, from the pressure to have sex, and safe from the pressure that may be inside us to just throw in the towel and do it.

When we're in a group, we'll still get a chance to meet people. We'll see how people act, and we'll have a chance to become friends with others. What we won't be is caught alone riding down lovers' lane, or somewhere else, where it will become very difficult for us to say no.

Determining to wait to date is all well and good, but what happens when we find ourselves falling into that swirling fog known as infatuation? Then the problem becomes the tugging of our own heartstrings. If we feel that we've embarked on a dangerous course, and can see that down the road we might lose our resolve to not have sex, then the best, most effective method to stop the multiplication of emotional love and sexual desire is to *manage the circumstances* of our relationship with the other person.

What does that mean? If we *really* want to wait to have sex, but feel a very strong emotional or sexual attraction, then the easiest way to avoid having sex is to not be alone with the other person.

We first have to ask ourselves some questions:

- Am I feeling sexually attracted to my one true love?

- Do I have a one true love, but am feeling attracted to someone else?

❧ Am I without a significant other, and just feel attracted
to someone whom I'm not yet serious about?

If the person to whom we're attracted is our one true love and we're not married yet, and if we both wish to save ourselves till marriage, then managing our circumstances is a temporary thing until that wonderful day when we tie the knot.

If our sexual attraction is directed toward someone else and we already have a significant other, then it becomes more serious, because we don't want to betray and hurt the one whom we already love. In that case, the safest and quickest way to avoid the incredible power of sexual attraction is to cut off from that person.

Cutting off from another person sounds cruel. We need to be aware, though, of the incredible power of love—even love that is misdirected. Our heart usually rules our intellect—so knowing that something is wrong just isn't enough if we've already fallen over the precipice of emotional or sexual attraction. In concrete terms, cutting off a relationship with another person might mean saying to that person, "I can't see you anymore, because I'm already committed to another."

Sometimes it's better to not say anything and just stop seeing the person, because speaking about it might make things worse. If the other person isn't attracted to us, then of course, we can't say anything at all.

Frankly, if more married men and women were aware of this method, there would be less infidelity. People often don't set out to be unfaithful—they just aren't aware of the way that emotional and sexual feelings multiply until they become overwhelming.

Cutting off a relationship is very, very difficult, but it is truly the best (and perhaps the only) way to protect yourself from illicit sexual relationships when your feelings of attraction get too strong. It will make it easier to do this if you confide in your parents and ask them for their help. They can give you moral support as well as external support. For example, if a boy or girl was really chasing you, and the situation became very troublesome, your parents could intervene.

If for some extreme reason you feel that you can't go to your parents, at least go to a responsible adult who can help you. The bottom line is, when you're in trouble, don't isolate yourself. Don't act alone. Get help at the beginning of a problem, when it's still small, rather than waiting until the end, when it might be overwhelming.

There are a lot of messages out there that "parents aren't cool," but you know what? Some of those people who in the 1960s said, "Never trust anyone over thirty" are now well past seventy! It happens to everyone. Just imagine life without your parents. I mean *really* without your parents. Wouldn't you be even a *tiny* bit sad? Our parents usually love us more than anyone else in the whole world. It's very smart (and the true love thing to do) to treat them like friends and allies. And we need allies, don't we?

Until we all resolve the conflict of desires that often roils inside us, it's safer and more realistic to say that none of us can trust our heart 100 percent. We can, however, trust our *circumstances.*

Here's a method that is worth repeating the proverbial three times. If we forget everything else, at least we should remember this:

- If we refuse to be alone with the person to whom we're attracted, it is unlikely that we'll have sex with him or her.

- If we refuse to be alone with the person to whom we're attracted, it is unlikely that we'll have sex with him or her.

- If we refuse to be alone with the person to whom we're attracted, it is unlikely that we'll have sex with him or her.

If we continually put ourselves in situations in which we're alone with that person, then our risk becomes much, much greater. If it all sounds too severe, take heart. True love is the most wonderful thing in the world, and is the ultimate destiny of every person—young and old.

Managing our circumstances also applies to our one true love, so that we can successfully wait until marriage to have sex. Someone might ask, "How do we get to know someone deeply if we're never alone together? How can we carry on deep and personal conversations with other people listening in?"

A simple method to balance the need to be careful with the practical need for privacy, to better get to know someone, is to sit together in a *partially* public setting. In other words, you don't have to discuss true love in the middle of the living room, surrounded by curious younger brothers or sisters who are making silly faces at you. Sit in the next room—with the door open—so that you can be seen but not heard. Or sit on the swing on the front porch (if you have a swing or a front porch). ☺ Pick a place that's public enough for safety, but private enough for a heart-to-heart talk.

So how do we find true love and avoid mistakes? In the next section we'll discuss practical methods called "Courtship 2.0."

But where does falling in love come into play? Let's be clear. Nobody wants to be condemned to a loveless marriage. Everyone wants to love and be loved. Living happily ever after is our eternal dream and the subject of countless stories and movies.

It's not really how a couple meets that is important. What's really important is what happens next. It's their mutual commitment to build a happy marriage, combined with their knowledge and wisdom about how to make their marriage work, that will help determine whether their marriage succeeds or fails.

After all, a husband or wife who fell madly in love with their honey and got married could then fall madly in love with someone else at any time. How many times have we seen that happen in Hollywood? Hormones, chemicals, and biological urges often combine with natural compatibility to trick people into thinking that they're in love, even though they still love their current spouse. How can we sort it out?

What will truly make a difference in marriage is when a husband and wife decide to make their marriage work by creating and deepening their mutual relationship of love. Committed and joyful love doesn't just happen. True love is created and maintained by unselfish and loving service. The wonderful thing is that the more we give and serve and love, the more we feel happy to do so.

Still, after meeting the potential love of one's life, one needs to find out if that person really is the one. Courting is a safe method to get to know the other person over a period of time—without sex. Courtship is a great way for girls to keep the wolves at bay. The rules of courtship are very simple. The girl makes sure that she hangs out in groups and in public settings, and when a boy tries to approach her with that clever smile we all know about, the girl ever so sweetly says, "Haven't you heard about courting? We have to get to know each other as friends first. Then we'll see where that goes."

And of course, the same thing applies when a girl approaches a boy. Friends first, and then we'll see.

Some doltish, insensitive people may laugh at the idea of courtship, but don't worry. Real, honorable, unselfish men love and admire women who are protective of themselves in this way. Don't listen to the mutterings of boys who are—at that moment—only thinking with their sexual organs. And if girls are the aggressors, then boys need to think more deeply about what they *truly* want.

It's true that teenagers often have to endure a certain amount of agony because of physical desires. The dilemma is that the desires of our body should never rule our unselfish heart—but unfortunately the desires of our body are often very strong. Which is why it can indeed be agonizing.

Yet in order to make an enduring and deep relationship of love with our future spouse, it's far healthier, from a spiritual point of view, to overcome sexual desire when it claws at us. How can we do that? One remedy is to be tough on our physical body. An effective method to overcome physical desire is to take a cold shower.

(Remember to check with your parents first!) It's also very important to walk away from things that have the wrong kind of stimulus, such as movies, television, books, or magazines that have sexual content.

Other at-risk behaviors, such as smoking, drinking, and drug use, tend to create an environment that can increase the risk of sexual activity. Therefore, the healthiest way of life is to avoid all of these at-risk behaviors. Not going to the latest wild party may sound horrendously dull, but in the long term, finding our one true love is much more exciting!

The best way to conquer our physical desires is to strengthen our emotional capacity to give and understand kind and compassionate love. Our body will yield to the higher power of unselfish love, because true love is the strongest power in the universe. Note that we said *true* love—not hormones or chemicals or infatuation. An example of our body obeying our unselfish heart is when we have the opportunity to give some of our lunch to someone who doesn't have enough. Our body will tell us to eat all of our food and not share it—but our heart knows otherwise.

The dilemma is that we lose touch with our deep heart quite frequently. We can stay in touch more easily with our true self through many methods, including daily reflection, prayer, meditation, or other types of soul-searching. The key is to do something every day to find "the real me" instead of the fake or confused version that sometimes creeps up on us, grabs us by the nose, and leads us down a thorny path.

The age of "teenagerdom" could be described as the period of "rampant desires." The fact that teenagers dream of true love is normal. Yet, teenagers with rampant desires still have to follow a road map, or they'll crash, like Mr. Toad in his roadster, in *The Wind in the Willows*. Then "the brutal minions of the law" (or, in this case, reality) will fall upon them. The road map we need to follow could also be called a "true love map"—a map that brings us back to the question of "dating or waiting."

Why should we hurry to date, anyway? Who wants to get pregnant (or get a girl pregnant) at sixteen or younger? Isn't it better to grow a bit and find out how we really feel about life? Waiting until we're older will give us a much better chance to learn how to love our spouse when we do get married.

At the same time, if two eighteen-year-olds decide to get married, with honor and respect and commitment, and a clear understanding of the road ahead of them, it's certainly better than living a promiscuous life. It's a toss-up between the huge difficulty of remaining abstinent and being mature enough to make our marriage work.

Becoming mature in our ability to love our spouse will also give us the ability to love our children when we have them. If teenagers date and have sex, they have to face the reality that girls do get pregnant—even if they use various precautions. Given that fact, it's very important to clarify once again that our goal is not just to reduce teenage pregnancies or eliminate sexually transmitted diseases. If those were our primary goals, then we would be talking about so-called safe sex and birth control methods. Many people would also say that the simple solution to unwanted teen pregnancies is abortion. Our discussion here takes the viewpoint that those methods miss the point entirely.

We're advocating *abstinence because of love*. Searching for ways to have safe sex, or contemplating having abortions, ignores the primary issue that the couple should not have sex until they're married and committed to building a lifelong relationship of true love. Transcendent love should be the primary ingredient of sex and the foundation for having children. From this point of view, abortions should never be needed. If couples waited to have sex until they were married and committed to each other, unwanted teen pregnancies or sexually transmitted diseases would no longer be an issue.

If teenagers do have sex before they're married, and then are faced with a pregnancy that they didn't plan, they are then in a very difficult position. From the point of view of true love, the only good option is for the couple to get married and raise their child with all the heart and love that they can muster. To not get married, and leave the mother to raise the child alone, or to abort the child because it's inconvenient, is a violation of heart. (There are of course exceptions, if one of the parents is unfit, or if there are other complex circumstances.)

It violates heart and true love because either action is essentially self-centered. It would be selfish for the father to abandon the mother and the child. The mother will say, "Where is the man who said that he loved me?" The child will say, "Where is my father? Why did he leave my mother and me?"

It would be selfish to abort the child, because the normal, original, and natural consequence of true love is a child. To abort a child because of inconvenience is to deny true love itself—not to mention the beautiful and wonderful life that the child should have. My wife once noted that the famous singers Celine Dion, Iris DeMent, and Enya were all the youngest of a large group of children in their respective families. What a loss to the world if their parents had aborted them!

The best solution for teenagers is to say "no" to sex before marriage, for the sake of their own happiness and for the sake of the children that they might have. If the teenage couple have children unexpectedly, they are obligated to raise them with true love and provide them with a loving home. If either the teenage father or mother tries to abandon the child, the other partner needs to seek help, from parents or counselors, in order to ensure that the child is raised properly. Adoption is truly the last resort. Children's normal, basic, commonsense point of view is that they want to be with their own parents. Nothing takes the place of our real parents, generally speaking.

Having children as teenagers is a huge task—for that reason, teenagers should wait to have children until their love is mature.

~ amok: *adv.* In or into an uncontrolled state or a state of extreme activity.

~ illicit: *adj.* Not sanctioned by custom or law; unlawful.

From the Text . . .

Some doltish, insensitive
people may laugh at the idea
of courtship, but don't worry.
Real, honorable, unselfish men
love and admire women who
are protective of themselves
in this way.

Don't listen to the mutterings
of boys who are—at that
moment—only thinking with
their sexual organs. And if girls
are the aggressors, then boys
need to think more deeply
about what they *truly* want.

Session Three
Roundtable Discussion Topics

1. Do teenagers have the intellectual capacity and the strength of moral will to say "no" to sex? Can an individual reject peer pressure and stand up for what he or she believes in?

2. No matter how much our hormones might be raging, and no matter how much pressure society places on us, isn't it true that deep down in our heart we believe that living a life of true, unselfish love is the best way to find happiness? Why is that true?

3. What is the best way to avoid pressure to have premarital sex?

4. Why is it so risky to be alone with a member of the opposite sex over a long period of time? Why do emotional feelings multiply when we have give and take with them?

5. Is the old-fashioned method of courting an option in today's society? If not, why not? Can public opinion about courting be changed in a positive direction?

6. Should the rules of courting apply equally to both males and females? Should parents be involved in monitoring dates and approving relationships? If not, why not?

7. What are some reasons that teenagers should save themselves until marriage and say no to sex? Why is that the true love thing to do?

Quotes to Live By
from Session Three

❧ It's time for teenagers to stand up and let people know that they're more than dumb animals run amok.

❧ It is possible to save our love for our spouse. Isn't it better to have pride in our inherent capability to be morally strong, intellectually clear, and concerned for the feelings of others? Insisting that sex should be saved for the one we'll love forever is the right thing to do, and the gutsy thing to do.

❧ The best defense against pressure from others to have casual and uncommitted sex is to look them in the eye, with a serious look, and say, "You believe in true, eternal love, don't you?" Who can say no to that? If they do say no, then you know that they're not the right person for you, anyway.

❧ If we refuse to be alone with the person to whom we're attracted, it is unlikely that we'll have sex with him or her.

∞ The age of "teenagerdom" could be described as the period of "rampant desires." The fact that teenagers dream of true love is normal. Yet, teenagers with rampant desires still have to follow a road map, or they'll crash, like Mr. Toad in his roadster, in *The Wind in the Willows*. Then "the brutal minions of the law" (or, in this case, reality) will fall upon them.

The road map we need to follow could also be called a "true love map"—a map that brings us back to the question of "dating or waiting."

∞ What will truly make a difference in marriage is when a husband and wife decide to make their marriage work by creating and deepening their mutual relationship of love. Committed and joyful love doesn't just happen. True love is created and maintained by unselfish and loving service.

The wonderful thing is that the more we give and serve and love, the more we feel happy to do so.

SESSION FOUR

Courtship 2.0

*Practical ways to find
the right marriage partner without
the emotional baggage of premarital sex*

Roundtable Discussions

Quotes to Live By

10-Minute Break

Courtship 2.0

*~ Practical ways to find
the right marriage partner without
the emotional baggage of premarital sex*

It's probably a safe bet that today's teenagers and young men and women never give a moment's thought to the words "courtship" and "courting." Young ladies who have seen Keira Knightley in her role as Elizabeth Bennet in the movie *Pride and Prejudice* might recognize the term, but only as a quaint tradition that has absolutely nothing to do with the twenty-first century.

One can hardly blame them. The idea of meeting Joey in the family parlor (assuming today's houses have a parlor) is hard enough to wrap one's mind around. To then have to put up with a chaperone and finally to ask one's parents for permission to marry is impossible to imagine for Western young people.

I don't recommend that we turn back the clock and revive courtship as it used to be. The many traditions connected to courtship are not necessarily good. Depending upon one's parents and requiring parental permission to marry, for example, can be a cause of great pain and tragedy. Historical courtship was far more complex than the simple dictionary definition of "the wooing of one person by another."

Yet I believe that some elements of courtship are worth reviving and reshaping into a new twenty-first-century tradition of courtship. Let's explore if "Courtship 2.0" can be a way to prevent marriage problems before they start, by finding the right marriage partner without the baggage of premarital sex.

Is the current method of finding a lifelong spouse working? Nowadays many preteens date and select boyfriends and girlfriends in a very casual way. Often unsatisfied after a short time, they unceremoniously dump the offending partner. Kissing, and more, is common at a very early age, with many teenagers engaging in oral sex as a way to have sex while declaring that they are "abstinent." Cohabitation, the practice of living together without the commitment of marriage, is common. Romance can become a shopping mall of "try before you buy" relationships, an arena where heartache is a frequent result.

Given the current environment in which young people are raised, I don't think that it's productive to judge anyone, least of all teenagers. How we, as a society, arrived at our current state of sexual and romantic standards is not the point. It is far more important for all of us, including all the teenagers and single persons who are seeking true love, to think independently and ask the right questions. Some young adults may say that they're not seeking true love and have no wish to be married. Some believe that it's perfectly fine to have casual sexual relationships.

I believe that *deep down* most people (if not all people) really do want to find someone whom they can love and who can love them. With that assumption, here are my recommendations for a new "Courtship 2.0."

The Two Pillars of Courtship 2.0

1. Find the Right Person for You

First, Courtship 2.0 is based on the view that you need to marry the right person *for you*. This isn't focused on money, status, or what society or anyone else thinks. Rather, this is centered on finding your soul mate—the person whom you can love for eternity and who can love you in return. Although you can potentially love anyone, finding the right person also means finding someone who is compatible with your mind and heart, your interests, your causes, your beliefs, and your value system. What kind of person do you want to wake up next to, fifty years from now?

Those who want to find a marriage partner should think deeply about what this means to them. It doesn't mean that falling in love is invalid; it doesn't mean that marriage should be reduced to "analysis." It simply means that a great deal of thought should go into what is arguably the most important step of one's life. This requires that you think about who you are, and what you like in life, before you can understand the kind of person you would like to marry.

Let me emphasize that I am *not* recommending that parents should be cut out of this exploratory process. Parents can be very helpful and save young people from dreadful mistakes. Certainly, if a person is underage, it is vital to seek help from one's parents.

2. Maintain Sexual Abstinence before Marriage

Second, in order to avoid all of the damage and baggage that are connected to premarital sex, Courtship 2.0 avoids premarital sexual activity completely, including oral sex and other sexual activities. It values long-term love and takes the view that sex is so precious and holy that it shouldn't be engaged in until after the commitment of marriage. This is based on the view that sex is *not* just physical but also has spiritual, emotional, and energetic components that affect the individuals involved.

If an individual's hope is to find his or her one true love and live happily ever after, then it's worth it to deeply examine the impact of having had many sexual partners before that lovely marriage ensues—versus the option of entering into that marriage as a virgin. As I wrote in the essay "Eternal Triune Marriage as a New Vision of Marriage" in the book *The Living Compass of Kindness and Compassionate Love*:

> Engaging in premarital sex, and casual sex with many partners, prevents a person from establishing the depth of transcendent sexual union that a person could potentially find with a committed and loving long-term partner.
>
> Casual sex is like a blindfolded visit to a spiritual garden that offers treasures that cannot be adequately perceived if one's focus is only on physical pleasure.
>
> Tragically, casual sex can damage a person's emotions and spirit to such a degree that the person's sensitivity to the spiritual luminescence of loving and transcendent sex is severely decreased. Everyone can be healed, without exception, but why go down paths that can damage us, when we don't have to?

Additional Guidelines for Courtship 2.0

3. Cultivate Friends Instead of a Boyfriend or Girlfriend and Make a New Tradition of No-Sex Dating

Until you're very sure, don't declare that anyone is your boyfriend or girlfriend. Thus there's no one to "dump."

Cultivate many friends in an effort to discover whom you would like to marry. Make sure that sex is not involved if you go on a date; this keeps your search for the perfect mate uncomplicated. Make a new tradition of No-Sex Dating.

4. Marry a Person
Who Will Be Your Dearest Friend

As you meet many potential marriage partners, look for the one who can be your dearest friend. Find out what makes them tick by talking deeply with them and watching them in action in their life. Discover their passions, their philosophies and ethics, and their heart and soul.

Find out if you are compatible with them by spending a great deal of non-sexual time with them. If they cannot be your dearest friend, then how could you live together in a happy marriage?

5. Make Sure That Your Future Spouse
Shares Your Views and Expectations
about Marriage

It's very important to talk at length with your potential spouse about his or her views on marriage. This includes views on man-woman relationships, including such topics as "Who's the boss?" (I think that "true love is the boss.")

Each of the partners has the right to maintain their autonomy as they seek to harmonize their lifestyles.

If the husband or wife wish to maintain certain activities, but find that their partner disapproves, that is an issue. Any two people who live together must bend a certain amount, so clarifying expectations in advance is the safest way to proceed. For example, what about child-rearing issues and careers? What about joint bank accounts? How do both parties feel about daily communication? What about sex? Both parties need to be on the same page *before* they get married.

Ensure that your future spouse agrees with you about the concepts of love—most especially about the importance of growing together toward a mutual resonance with the highest qualities of kindness and compassionate love. If one partner believes in God and has a spiritual viewpoint about marriage but the other partner does not, the dichotomy may be rough going as your marriage experiences the stresses of life.

6. You Can Marry a Flawed Person, But Don't Marry a Person Whose Lifestyle Violates Your Conscience

We're all flawed, so marrying a flawed person is a given. Our idols *will* have feet of clay. Expecting our spouse to not have flaws is unreasonable and unrealistic. To make a marriage work, we'll have to love our spouse in spite of his or her flaws and hope that they do the same for us.

Yet we should not marry a person whose lifestyle violates our conscience, that is, someone who is living their life in a bad way. You will have to define what "bad" means to you. Criminals are usually included in this category—which does *not* mean that those individuals can't turn their lives around. Sometimes true love is all it takes. However, marrying someone in order to "save them" is a course fraught with risk and emotional pain, and sometimes with physical danger. We should not marry someone who might abuse us, either physically or emotionally, either publicly or privately.

As a boy, George Washington copied down the maxim ". . . 'tis better to be alone than in bad Company."[1] If this is true for normal acquaintances, how much more is it true for our eternal mate?

7. Make Sure That Both of You Commit to Each Other 100 Percent

For richer, for poorer, in good times and bad really means something. You *will* fight—some couples more than others. Can you both commit to loving each other in spite of your flaws, beyond any limitations? Can you both commit to never divorcing and to staying together, no matter what? Commitment becomes vitally important when you have children.

Do you want to commit to marriage only until "death parts you" or would you like to commit to the newer vision of marriage that continues after death? An eternal commitment provides the most strength in a marriage, because both parties gain a long-term perspective based on their belief that they will be together "a thousand years from now" (and more) and will have time to grow, improve, and mature. Of course, this type of commitment is not *a law*. You don't need to think, "Oh no, if I commit like that, what if it really doesn't work out after all? Am I stuck forever?"

You are *not stuck*, because every person must have the freedom to follow their heart when it comes to marriage. Love cannot be forced. The central theme of making a marriage commitment is that we should not be *casual* about marriage. It's worth it to give it our best shot and really, really try to make it work. If your spouse turns out to be a truly horrible person, or if it becomes clear that there's no way the marriage will work after all, then sometimes divorce is the only solution.

8. Enter Marriage with a Maintenance Plan: Communicate, Communicate, Communicate

Decide in advance to communicate on a deep, internal level every day, before and after you're married. Maintaining a healthy marriage is Job Number One for married couples, for it affects their children, their daily joy, their inspiration, their finances, and innumerable other areas of their lives. It takes work, committed love, service, and complete and constant honesty about internal and external issues. Communication during marriage is, in every sense of the phrase, a "maintenance plan."

⋙ ⋙ ⋙

Are the above guidelines for Courtship 2.0 realistic for today's teenagers, young people, and older singles? I believe they are. Some of them may be controversial—but people interested in finding their one true love don't need to shrink from controversy.

In the end, getting married is something that each person has to come to terms with by themselves (and when one is young, with help from one's parents whenever possible). Still, when we reach adulthood, we are under no obligation to anyone when it comes to marriage, except to ourselves, our spouse and children, and, if you feel so inclined to believe, to God. Marriage, perhaps more than any other pursuit, deserves the phrase "To thine own self be true."

1. Conway, Moncure D.
*George Washington's Rules of Civility:
Traced to their Sources and Restored*
New York: Hurst & Company, 1890

From the Text . . .

Courtship 2.0 is based on the view that you need to marry the right person *for you.*

This isn't focused on money, status, or what society or anyone else thinks. Rather, this is centered on finding your soul mate—the person whom you can love for eternity and who can love you in return.

Session Four
Roundtable Discussion Topics

1. Is the current method of finding a lifelong spouse working?

2. How important is it to find the right person to love and possibly marry? What are some methods that we can use to find the right person?

3. Is it possible that having sex with just one committed partner will allow us to experience a deeper and more transcendent relationship than if we have sex with many different partners? If so, why is this?

4. Is it a good idea to develop many platonic friendships before we look for a boyfriend or girlfriend, so that we can discover the right person for us?

5. Will it make a difference in our future marriage if we marry a person who shares many or even most of our interests, values, and views about life?

6. How important is it that both persons make a mutual commitment to the marriage?

7. Will it make a difference if both persons actively communicate about both internal and external things, before and after the marriage?

Quotes to Live By
from Session Four

❧ Courtship 2.0 is based on the view that you need to marry the right person *for you*. This isn't focused on money, status, or what society or anyone else thinks. Rather, this is centered on finding your soul mate—the person whom you can love for eternity and who can love you in return.

❧ Casual sex is like a blindfolded visit to a spiritual garden that offers treasures that cannot be adequately perceived if one's focus is only on physical pleasure.

❧ As you meet many potential marriage partners, look for the one who can be your dearest friend. Find out what makes them tick by talking deeply with them and watching them in action in their life. Discover their passions, their philosophies and ethics, and their heart and soul. Find out if you are compatible with them by spending a great deal of non-sexual time with them. If they cannot be your dearest friend, then how could you live together in a happy marriage?

৵ It's very important to talk at length with your potential spouse about his or her views on marriage. . . . Both parties need to be on the same page before they get married.

৵ For richer, for poorer, in good times and bad really means something. You will fight—some couples more than others. Can you both commit to loving each other in spite of your flaws, beyond any limitations?

৵ Decide in advance to communicate on a deep, internal level every day, before and after you're married. Maintaining a healthy marriage is Job Number One for married couples.

৵ Marriage, perhaps more than any other pursuit, deserves the phrase "To thine own self be true."

SESSION FIVE

Becoming a Person of True Love and Preparing to Have Children

Building a Marriage of True Love

Roundtable Discussions

Quotes to Live By

Becoming a Person of True Love and Preparing to Have Children

Although children are the result of their parents making love to each other, it is a terribly tragic fact that all too often the parents don't love each other or their children enough. After we get married and have children, how can we ensure that our children will grow up to become men and women of unselfish and parental love? Isn't it true that in order to understand unselfish love to the point of being able to give it to others, a person must receive adequate parental love first? How can someone give to others what they have never experienced?

From this point of view, our responsibility as future parents is serious indeed. When a young man and young woman fall in love, they can't ignore the topic of children. The ultimate, original result of the love of a husband and wife is a child. How, then, will their love influence the life of the child to be?

Let's assume that the husband and wife have decided to have a child, and the wife is not yet pregnant. What kind of child will be born from the couple? Just as it is obvious that certain trees produce a certain quality of fruit, doesn't it make sense that a child will reflect the heart, love, spirit, and character of the father and mother?

It is not only the training of the child during his or her childhood years that will influence the child. The very nature or character of the parents at the moment of conception will be embedded in the core of the child's character. The internal inheritance of character and heart is similar to the external inheritance of certain physical features that the child will bear.

The concept of "education in the womb" illustrates the sensitivity of a child to the atmosphere of harmony and love that is present in the home, and between husband and wife, even before the child is born. Some forward-thinking doctors recommend that women who are pregnant listen to beautiful music so that the child in their womb can develop a deep sensitivity to beauty.

It becomes the burden (although it's also a labor of love) of the new couple to make a sincere effort to grow in their ability to love parentally, even before their child is conceived. This is an additional reason why young men and women should wait to have sex until they're married and have matured adequately. If a young, immature girl has a baby, how will she love her child when she is still a child herself?

❧ ❧ ❧

Building a marriage of true love with our future spouse and raising children with parental love both require that we, as future fathers or mothers, prepare ourselves and train ourselves to become men and women of unselfish love. Unfortunately, becoming a person of true love is usually not something that is taught in school. Young people often find themselves married, with a child on the way, before they have had a chance to gain a clear concept of marriage and parenting.

Marriages often fail miserably because the husband and wife don't know how to care for each other and therefore don't take the necessary steps to deepen their relationship of love. After thirty years, they look at each other and realize that they no longer love—or even like—each other. The tragedy is that the distance between them is not what they started with, and is something that might have been completely avoided.

After the couple marry, parenting is far more than learning how to change diapers, feed the baby, and provide a comfortable living environment for the child. A child will grow up, perhaps physically well taken care of, and still wonder, "Do my father and mother love me?"

One of the beautiful aspects of unselfish love is that it cuts across all areas of our life. Just as unselfish love is so essential to a successful marriage and a wholesome sexual relationship, unselfish love is the primary qualification to be a parent. It makes life simple, in a way, for we can focus our heart and mind on a very beautiful, simple, yet strong credo to love others unselfishly.

But our task is not easy, is it? As teenagers, we may still be struggling to understand ourselves, and life in general, and still be wondering if we'll ever find our own true love. In the midst of all that, without much guidance, we must train ourselves to create a beautiful marriage and to become a good parent.

One might think that it's all vastly unfair, or entirely too quick for us to grasp everything in time to care for our future spouse and children adequately. In a way, our situation as we grow up throughout our teens is really too difficult. Part of the problem is that human history has been a history of people having children before they were ready and able to love them properly, so that those children couldn't receive adequate love or training. Each generation of children has been caught in the vicious cycle of being unready and ill-prepared to have their own children.

Today's young people are in a special situation. Although the pressures of life might seem greater than ever, with the world becoming smaller every day and the pace of life getting faster and faster, the opportunities to grow in new ways are unprecedented in human history.

Because the world is within each person's reach, and because cultures and other forms of knowledge are being shared throughout the world, young people have the chance to develop their heart of compassion and true love in a deeper and more profound way than earlier generations. Young people have a chance today to establish new standards of true love and heart, no matter what field of endeavor or career they commit themselves to.

By vigorously striving to become a person of true love, we will be able to care for our future husband or wife and our children, as well as our friends, our families, and our associates. It's really important to ask ourselves what kind of person we want to become. Besides deciding on our career goal or external life's ambition, we need to clarify our internal goal as a person. Two people can grow up and become successful, and one will be selfish and corrupt, and the other will be generous, humble, serving, and loving toward others. Which do we want to become?

Isn't it an admirable goal to say, "I want to become a person who can give and serve and love on a daily basis?" Yet, how many of your friends have that goal, think like that, or even talk about living that way? If we don't lock onto that target, becoming a person of true love will be a long shot at best. It's just too easy to be selfish.

Mother Teresa once wrote, in a letter to the sisters of the Missionaries of Charity:

> Let no one ever come to you without coming away better, happier. Be the living expression of God's kindness. Everybody should see kindness in your face, in your eyes, in your smile, in your warm greeting.[1]

What a beautiful goal! Becoming a person of kindness and true love is a gradual process that requires a lot of thought and reflection. It requires digging into ourselves with humility, to find both the good and bad parts of our character. When we find a bad spot in our heart or mind, we can act as our own spiritual and emotional doctor and cut out the bad spots with the invisible scalpel of true love.

Having a realistic view of ourselves will give us the strength to be humble, and to apologize to others when we hurt them. All too often, saying sorry is an ability that is woefully absent from our life as we grow up. The courage to apologize to others will allow us to look our future spouse in the eye and take responsibility for the quality of our love.

The quality of our love is the central factor in determining the success of our marriage. It's not really our future spouse who will be the problem. Oh, it's true that our spouse will have his or her own responsibility to be a person of true love. But our ability to give love is what we must focus on. This is one of the reasons why preparing ourselves for marriage is the true love thing to do. Saving ourselves until marriage gives us a chance to grow in our quality of love for others, so that when we do get married, we'll be more prepared to give our spouse true love through thick and thin.

Then, as a future husband or wife, and parent, with a clear vision of the beauty and value of unselfish love, we will continue to develop in a good way. We'll be able to love our children and teach our children to grow properly and become wonderful children of true love in their own right. We will have become a "person of true love," with a husband or wife of true love and children of true love, forming a beautiful family of true love. What could be more inspiring?

1. Mother Teresa of Calcutta
in a letter written in May, 1964 to
the sisters of the Missionaries of Charity

The writings of Mother Teresa of Calcutta
© by the Mother Teresa Center, exclusive licensee
throughout the world of the Missionaries of Charity
for the works of Mother Teresa.
Used with permission.

Building a Marriage of True Love

The first step in preparing ourselves for marriage is the preservation of the beautiful and unspoiled heart of love that we had as children. Loving our future husband or wife in a complete and mature way will be difficult if our heart is tired and bruised from numerous relationships prior to our marriage. Saving ourselves until marriage avoids the baggage and pain that often are created when people engage in premarital sex.

Although some people live together before marriage as a way of testing the relationship, the long-term negative effects of "living together" are often overlooked. One of the problems of living together without the commitment of marriage is that the relationship between the man and woman often lacks the key ingredient of commitment that helps a marriage endure. With the knowledge that their experiment of living together may end at any time, the partners often place divisions between important elements of their lives, such as bank accounts or house ownership.

When difficulties in their relationship arise, it's easy to say, "Hit the road, Jack," or "Scram, Maybellene." Instead of being "good practice" for marriage, living together can develop habits and attitudes that make a committed marriage even harder. "Starter marriages," which are based on the concept that one needs practice before a final, long-term marriage, are as damaging as living together. A couple's long-term, mutual commitment to a successful marriage, through all the difficulties of life, is the foundation to build a marriage of true love. Anything less than total commitment makes a marriage a strong candidate for failure.

When the husband and wife share a common set of values or spiritual beliefs, their path is even smoother, for their commitment gains the fuel of a shared motivation of heart. The beliefs and values of husbands and wives are sometimes all over the map, opening up the possibility of disagreements and conflict. In searching for a common ground that cuts across barriers, couples may wish to adopt the "true love thing to do" as a way of life. The essence of the "true love thing to do" way of life is the belief that expressing unselfish love to others is the best way to live.

When "True Love Is the Boss" for both the husband and wife, it becomes easier to resolve conflicts as they arise. Doesn't it make sense that a husband, however macho he may be, should bow to the beauty of true love? If his wife is more loving than he is at any particular moment, shouldn't he humbly listen to her? When both the husband and wife hold true love itself in the highest regard, conflicts will happen less frequently.

When the husband says to himself, "I must love more; I must give more; I must serve more," and then makes effort every day to do so, his path in marriage will become smoother. When the wife feels and acts in the same way, the marriage is well on its way to becoming a happy one.

Love is a creative power that multiplies with every ounce of effort poured into its application. In a way, true love is like exercise—the more emotional weights that we try to lift, the easier it gets. Love given to our spouse, in this way, becomes a wonderful "road" that we want to stay on forever. If we declare to ourselves that we'll "give and love and serve" infinitely, going beyond our own concepts or limitations, we'll discover that the power of love can crumble any barrier.

It's important to realize that in marriage there are indeed barriers to true love. Some of them are ancestral or historical—such as the "ancient rage" that many women feel, under the surface, because of the mistreatment of women by men throughout the ages. Ancient rage may be a new and uncomfortable concept for some men—but it's not too difficult to review the multitude of ways in which men have abused women in history. Unfortunately, historical "baggage" often becomes a stumbling block in marriage and thus needs to be dealt with by both the husband and wife.

Historical pain can also surface when a man and woman from former enemy countries, or different races or religions, fall in love and marry. Even though the husband and wife may not have participated in those historical conflicts, they may sometimes feel the burden of historical pain or resentment. Of course, their families may also have difficulties digesting their marriage.

Someone might say that it's better to not marry across the boundaries of race, religion, or historical enmity. However, building a marriage of true love across enemy lines is perhaps the best way to contribute to a world of true peace. It has been demonstrated in history, over and over again, that love in marriage has the power to resolve the conflicts between opposing sides.

The immigrants in New York City experienced this a hundred years ago. As each new wave of immigrants came to New York, conflicts would arise between the newest group and the ones already in residence. After a while, they would start marrying each other, and the conflicts would subside—until the next group came ashore.

The children of interracial couples have a special power that only grandchildren have. Even if the granddaddy is a bigot, there's something devastatingly cute about the little grandchild sitting on his knee. The smile of a child breaks racial barriers down.

If a man and woman enter into marriage committed to "love their enemy," beyond their own suffering, sacrifice, or death, then the power of their sacrificial love will create a marriage that has the potential to endure forever. It might seem unnecessary to commit oneself in such an extreme way, when couples are usually not enemies and in fact are usually in love with each other. Will it really be so tough? Does one need to prepare for so much sacrifice and service? Marriage might begin to sound like a very unpleasant option for a young man or woman contemplating a life together. Where's the joy in marriage? Where's the true love?

One of the core issues of marriage—or any relationship, for that matter, is what to do when problems arise. How do we conduct ourselves when our husband or wife gets cranky, or irrational, or selfish, or mean, or lazy, or leaves hair in the sink, or spends too much money, or does one of a million other things that tend to create feelings in us that could be summed up as: "My spouse is acting badly and not loving me enough"?

The selfish behavior of our spouse affects us where it hurts—our heart. We don't feel loved when our spouse is inconsiderate or selfish. When we don't feel loved, a common chain of reactions is to feel hurt, get angry, and then get even by being mean right back. Thus, "baggage" is created between the couple. The atmosphere of love, sweet love is blown to bits by the chill winds of anger and resentment and complaint.

Many marriages follow the route of baggage accumulation. The couple fall totally in love. They get married. They have children. They have debts and bills and pressures. Daily life hits them in the face. When they argue, they don't make up very well. Emotional baggage starts to collect after years of being swept under the rug. After ten, then twenty, then thirty years, they realize that the burning sparks of passion and love have been squelched by thousands of little incidents of mutual mistreatment. Tired, bitter, and angry, the couple that once were in love end their marriage in divorce.

Building a marriage of true love requires thousands of brave smiles. It requires thousands of moments of biting our tongue, gulping a bit, and giving love to our spouse—even though, at that moment, our spouse may have hurt us.

When we digest the pain caused by our spouse, and then give anyway, serve anyway, and love anyway, the pain caused by our spouse doesn't escalate. Loving endlessly in this fashion requires effort and patience and the long-range vision that someday, if enough effort is made, we will be in complete harmony with our spouse, centered on love. Of course, it may not be our spouse who is causing the pain at any particular moment—we ourselves almost certainly will be to blame many times.

If our spouse is less mature or less loving than we are, then we who are "more loving" (at least in our own mind) are placed in the inevitable position of loving our spouse with a forgiving and compassionate heart. Otherwise, we wouldn't be more loving than our spouse, would we? Isn't logic amazing?

The good news is that giving kind and compassionate love, or parental love, to one's husband or wife is a joyful process. Expressing true love requires humility and the realization that even if one seems "better" or more mature than the other, we're not really that good, compared to the *highest* possible standard of unselfish love.

Since the purpose of giving love is to make the other person happy, which makes us happy, then the real secret of giving love appears in front of our nose—we love giving true love to our husband or wife because the mutual relationship of love that develops becomes the source of intense and ever-expanding joy. Once we experience the joy that comes from giving true love, we want to give love again and again and again.

The time to multiply and maintain a beautiful atmosphere of heart is when the couple begin their married life, before the living room carpet of their life has mounds of secret pain swept under it. The problem with sweeping things under the rug is that the dirt and trash created by quarrels and arguments don't stay hidden. The piles get so big eventually that the husband and wife sometimes trip over them like explosive land mines.

Maintaining an atmosphere of heart is very much like weeding a garden. When an argument springs up, then the couple need to stop and pull it out of their garden of heart like the weed that it is. Tending their garden of heart is a job that needs daily attention. Weeds and bugs are sneaky, and so are the seeds of conflict. Conflict can start in a moment, over terribly mundane and boring things like dirty laundry on the floor and "Where's my dinner!?"

Removing the weeds of hurt and misunderstanding when they're still weeds can only happen if the husband and wife communicate constantly. True love and harmony are difficult to maintain if the couple don't understand each other's heart and mind and thoughts and dreams. If they're strangers to each other in their heart and mind, then how close will their relationship of true love become?

Yet, how many husbands and wives communicate frequently and effectively? One of the purposes of communication is understanding. With more and more couples coming from diverse backgrounds and cultures, communication is essential to understanding the thoughts and feelings of a spouse who might have been raised with a radically different life experience or world-view.

Some cultures consider verbal communication about matters of the heart unnecessary, based on the view that husbands and wives should be able to understand each other's heart and mind without words. Spiritual and intuitive understanding and communication are natural in those cultures, perhaps because of hundreds of years of shared experience that fosters easy understanding. However, the ability to understand someone without words does not change the fact that understanding itself is the goal—it doesn't really matter how we understand each another.

The "bottom line," so to speak, is rather simple: If a husband and wife don't understand each other, for whatever reason, communication becomes necessary. If words are required, so be it.

There's a book called *Men Are from Mars, Women Are from Venus*. What if men and women really were from Mars and Venus? They certainly would have to make a great deal of effort to understand each other. They couldn't possibly demand that the other party understand them without words. The easiest way to look at the need for communication is very practical: If either the husband or wife feels that they are misunderstood, or don't understand the other, they should insist that they sit down and talk. And talk and talk and talk, for hours and days and weeks and years (not all at one stretch, of course), until they understand each other more.

Sometimes, the husband and/or wife doesn't want to talk. It might not be in their nature to express things deeply, or frequently. Men often find it difficult to communicate about mushy things like "love" and "heart." It seems too feminine to men, or "sissified." Because of this, many women feel that men are underdeveloped in their ability to express love or give love to others—and deficient in their ability to talk about true love.

Are women right? It's up to men in the twenty-first century (the century that may become known as the "Age of Illumination") to prove to their wives that they can give true love to others and communicate sincerely about true love. And why not? True love and sacrificial love can be masculine as well as feminine. When a firefighter risks his life to save a child in a burning building, his actions may very well reflect his internal heart of love for others. What's wrong with talking about it? Absolutely nothing! Hey, guys, are you listening?

When either the husband or wife finds it difficult to communicate, then it makes a huge difference in the marriage if the partner who communicates more easily takes the initiative to guide and help the other spouse to communicate about internal things. It might be difficult in the beginning, but the "communicator" shouldn't give up in his or her efforts to reach into the heart and dreams of their spouse and find the place where the couple can touch each other's hearts.

That invisible place where the husband and wife meet with their heart is their resting place and the center of their home. They can breathe there, and their children can be safe there. Home really is where the heart is.

Eventually, the husband and wife will feel so close that they are happiest when they're together. Living together in sincerity and trust, they won't joke about "taking a break from the spouse." Being together will be as natural as breathing.

No matter how much or how little love the husband and wife feel toward each other at the beginning of their marriage, the critical factor for their success is that they make the effort to build a marriage of true love from the moment that they leave the altar. Even a couple who are madly in love will encounter rough spots that might derail their marriage in the future. Their mutual commitment to creatively multiply and deepen their relationship of love will guide them over the rough spots.

It takes patience and effort, but creating a marriage of true love is not only possible, it's every person's right. Even though many young people are nervous about marriage, and are experimenting with living together first, can't we assume that everyone wants to find "their one true love"? Even old, sourpuss hermits living in the mountains must feel lonely, since they don't have their soul mate next to them, with beautiful children and grandchildren sharing their holidays. In the ideal sense, families complete us and make our lives whole. That's why grandparents will sometimes refer to their many grandchildren as a "blessing" that they've received.

In the same way, marriage is also a blessing—a blessing that's completed by the couple as they build an eternal relationship of love.

Today's young people have the opportunity to be the pioneers of a new "marriage culture" that lifts up the beauty and value of eternal marriages centered on true love. Marriages of this type will transform society, especially when the marriages are between different races, cultures, religions, and nationalities.

Children raised in families based on marriages of true love will learn from their parents how to give true, unselfish love to their brothers and sisters, and thus to other people when they get older. Families like this will become the "school of love" for the children. The world is complicated, but when we boil everything down to the most basic unit of society, we find the individual, the husband and wife, and children: the family.

When a husband and wife pledge to each other that they will love each other without limitation, and together love their children, and then with their children strive to love and serve the world, the ripple effect across society and the world will contribute to an atmosphere of peace. Combined with other families who are living in the same way, we can say that marriages and families of true love are the building blocks of a peaceful world.

The twenty-first century can indeed become the Age of Illumination—but it will partially depend upon each husband and wife searching for the higher ground of true love that is burning in each person's heart, waiting to expand and multiply into a culture of kindness and a world of peace. Building marriages of true love will change the world.

From the Text . . .

Marriages often fail miserably
because the husband and wife
don't know how to care for each
other and therefore don't take
the necessary steps to deepen
their relationship of love.

From the Text . . .

After thirty years, they look at
each other and realize that
they no longer love—or even
like—each other.

The tragedy is that the
distance between them is not
what they started with, and is
something that might have
been completely avoided.

Session Five
Roundtable Discussion Topics

1. Is it better to wait to have children until we are at least eighteen, so that we are more mature in our love, and better able to take care of them? How are children, families, and society affected by a large number of unwanted pregnancies?

2. Do we want to become men and women of true love? How can we train ourselves to become a person of true love?

3. Is it easier to become a person who cares for others, and gives, serves, and loves on a daily basis, if we establish that as a clear, written goal? If we don't have internal goals, how will our future be affected?

4. Why is ongoing communication so important in marriage?

5. Is the ability to give unselfish love to our future spouse one of the most important ingredients for a successful marriage? What are some other ingredients for a happy marriage?

6. What are some of the reasons that marriages fail? How can we prevent the breakdown of our marriage in the future?

7. How will building marriages of true love affect peace in the world? Will it help create a world of peace if couples from different races, cultures, and nationalities marry? If so, why is that true?

Quotes to Live By from Session Five

≪ If a young, immature girl has a baby, how will she love her child when she is still a child herself?

≪ Human history has been a history of people having children before they were ready and able to love them properly, so that those children couldn't receive adequate love or training. Each generation of children has been caught in the vicious cycle of being unready and ill-prepared to have children.

≪ Marriages often fail miserably because the husband and wife don't know how to care for each other and therefore don't take the necessary steps to deepen their relationship of love. After thirty years, they look at each other and realize that they no longer love—or even like—each other. The tragedy is that the distance between them is not what they started with, and is something that might have been completely avoided.

❧ If we declare to ourselves that we'll "give and love and serve" infinitely, going beyond our own concepts or limitations, we'll discover that the power of love can crumble any barrier.

❧ Mother Teresa once wrote, in a letter to the sisters of the Missionaries of Charity: "Let no one ever come to you without coming away better, happier. Be the living expression of God's kindness. Everybody should see kindness in your face, in your eyes, in your smile, in your warm greeting."

❧ Isn't it an admirable goal to say, "I want to become a person who can give and serve and love on a daily basis?" Yet, how many of your friends have that goal, think like that, or even talk about living that way? If we don't lock onto that target, becoming a person of true love will be a long shot at best. It's just too easy to be selfish.

❧ The essence of the "true love thing to do" way of life is the belief that expressing unselfish love to others is the best way to live. When "True Love Is the Boss" for both the husband and wife, it becomes easier to resolve conflicts as they arise.

❧ Building marriages of true love will change the world.

Online Links

Web Page of Book and Publisher's Email

Information about the book is listed here:

https://worldcommunitypress.com/tl

The publisher's email is:

publishers@worldcommunitypress.com

Online Evaluation Form

The online evaluation form is at:

https://worldcommunitypress.com/tl/evaluation

Moderators and participants can fill out the evaluation form, if they wish, to provide feedback and suggestions about the workbook, as well as to provide any comments or quotes about the text and the seminar experience.

Graduation Certificate

The graduation certificate is at:

https://worldcommunitypress.com/tl/certificate

Moderators are encouraged to print the certificate and present it to each student after graduation.

Telling Others about the Book and Seminar

You are invited to tell others about the book and seminar. In fact, you can make a very substantial commission on sales of the book to groups. For more information, visit the link below:

https:/worldcommunitypress.com/tl/salesreps

Booking the Author as a Public Speaker

Peter Falkenberg Brown is available for public speaking bookings. His topics include *The True Love Thing to Do*, as well as many topics related to the themes of love, beauty, joy, and freedom. Videos of his speeches and presentations are at his "Love, Freedom, & the World Video Channel" at:

peterfalkenbergbrown.com/youtube

For more information please visit his web page or email him at the address below.

https://peterfalkenbergbrown.com/public-speaking/

peterbrown@worldcommunity.com

About the Author

It's common for "About the Author" sections to be very short bits of prose written in the third person. I've never seen one that included photos, as this one does. I've decided to break the rules and not only include photos but also write this section in the first person, and write more than a little snippet.

Although David Copperfield began his story with the chapter heading "I Am Born," I shall refrain from telling you that I was born under a canoe on Miami Beach while the moon gazed sympathetically at my mother as she was pelted with coconuts by monkeys howling in the palm trees.

I cannot say that my birth happened that way, for it did not, since I was instead born in a hospital in Coral Gables, Florida, in 1954, two months premature. It was quite unexciting but not dull, at least from my mother's point of view.

My mother, Polly Kapteyn Brown, was my best friend throughout my childhood. Although she was not a "huggy" type of person, she was someone whom I could trust and love and respect.

I arrived in life in the footsteps of my ancestors, starting with my parents. I owe them a profound debt for the goodness and merit that they left behind. In particular, my mother believed in my potential and gave me the vision, while I was still young, to try to think on a grand philosophical scale. (I am still attempting to do that.) Polly was an artist and art teacher, first at the Portland School of Fine and Applied Arts (the precursor to MECA, the Maine College of Art) and then at a school called "Concept" that she founded with some fellow artists, including the noted Maine artist Bill Manning. In 1982, a year before she died from lung cancer, she earned a graduate degree from the Episcopal Divinity School in Cambridge, Massachusetts.

She was also a writer, poet, and philosopher, perhaps inspired by her aunt, and my grandaunt, Olga Fröbe-Kapteyn, a Dutch spiritualist, theosophist, and scholar. Olga was the founder of the Eranos Foundation in Ascona, Switzerland, and was a friend of Carl Gustav Jung's.

Olga was in turn inspired by her mother, and my great-grandmother, Geertruida Agneta Kapteyn-Muysken, a humanist and leading social activist in nineteenth-century London. She was influenced by the French poet and philosopher Jean-Marie Guyau and counted George Bernard Shaw and Prince Pyotr Alexeyevich Kropotkin among her large circle of friends. She was an influential writer in London for twenty years and then moved to Zurich, where she became the center of a group of artists and students. Many Polish and Russian student émigrés regarded her as their "spiritual mother."[1]

This lineage of writers was unknown to me when I was a student. I believed that it was from my mother alone that I had inherited my passion for writing. I was thus quite fascinated when I learned more about the lives of Olga and Geertruida.

My confidence to follow a writing career was also bolstered in my high school days, when my senior-class English teacher at the Waynflete School in Portland, the late William Ackley, said to me, "Brownie, you've got it.

1. MUYSKEN, Geertruida Agneta. BWSA - Biografisch Woordenboek van het. Socialisme en de Arbeidersbeweging in Nederland. https://socialhistory.org/bwsa/biografie/muysken Web page viewed on December 10, 2016

Keep going!" (Or something to that effect.) I kept going, and am immensely grateful for his encouragement.

I am indeed fortunate to have met and married a wonderful lady who is also a writer and spiritualist, my dear bride, Kimmy Sophia. I affectionately call her "the Forest Queen." For a number of years now, we have co-published *The Significato Journal*, an online magazine with the theme "nectar for the soul" and an emphasis on the arts, nature, spirituality, and service. The magazine is at significatojournal.com. We reside in my home state of Maine, and have four children, all in their twenties.

My father, Carl Falkenberg Brown, was the son of Norman Brown of Portland, Maine, and the Baroness Helen Dean Falkenberg, of Quebec City. "Granny" and her four siblings each inherited their titles from their father, Baron Fredrick

Andreas Falkenberg, since their family received the title

in 1733, starting with my seventh great-grandfather Baron Conrad von Falkenberg of Trystorp, Sweden, and thus by Swedish law did not follow the tradition of primogeniture.

Carl was the great-grandson of William Wentworth Brown, who developed the Brown Paper Company in the late 1860s in Berlin, New Hampshire. Second great-grandfather William (known as "W.W.") was the son of a farmer, Jonathan, born in 1776 in Hallowell, Maine.

Jonathan was a devout Christian and held Bible studies in the family home in Clinton, Maine, for forty years. Jonathan's lineage started in America with the arrival in Boston of my seventh great-grandfather William Browne, where he married my seventh great-grandmother Elizabeth Ruggles in 1655.

William came from Dunfermline, Scotland, and may have emigrated to America to avoid Oliver Cromwell's armies, which was ironic, considering that my seventh great-granduncle on my grandmother's side was the ruthless and infamous Charles Fleetwood, commander in chief of Cromwell's armies.

William Wentworth Brown built a company that thrived for almost seventy years, until the Great Depression and off-shore competition ended its run. At its height, the Brown Paper Company owned four million acres of timberland and had turned tiny Berlin into a thriving town.

W.W. and his sons built a company that was known for its honesty, and its kindness to its employees and the residents of Berlin. Although the family failed to surmount the challenges of the Depression, a family historian wrote that when they failed, they "failed honorably."

By the time I was born, the Brown money was long gone, leaving my father to struggle and scrape and do his best to raise three children. Since we were poor, our family often returned to live in Granny's house, a large brick manse at 135 Vaughan Street in Portland's prosperous West End. Of all the many places in which I lived as a child, my grandmother's house was the one that I counted as home.

I've often reflected that growing up "poor" might have been for the best, since who knows what kind of person I would have been if I had

been raised in wealth? Life is full of mysteries like that, but I am truly happy that the "wealthy Browns" believed in kindness and honesty and honor. To my mother, most especially, I am grateful that I inherited a deep love for writing and art and nature and music and all things of beauty. I've discovered that being surrounded by those things throughout my life gave me the experiential knowledge that I was the very opposite of poor.

I inherited an adventurous spirit from my ancestors, and when I was eighteen, in 1973, I rode off into the sunset on a bicycle, headed for the Mardi Gras in New Orleans, and  then on to California. I spent two weeks traveling through the back roads of New England until I arrived at the Connecticut-New York border. Much to my surprise, after visiting my paternal aunt in New York City, I decided to stay, and live in Manhattan.

My bicycle trip had been contemplative and had heightened my sense that I was on a spiritual search. I had kept a picture of Jesus next to my bed since I was four years old, and had been inspired by books like *The Robe* by Lloyd C. Douglas, about a Roman soldier who gambled for Jesus' robe, converted to Christianity, and then died a martyr under Roman arrows. I had a strong desire to follow Jesus, and wished that I could have been alive when he preached in Israel. My mother had also introduced me to other religious avenues, and as I arrived in New York in my quest to "go west, young man," I was busily reading books by Erich Fromm, J. Krishnamurti, and various Sufi authors.

I stayed in New York for a couple of years, and then began a long process of exploring the rest of the country. Along the way, I became a writer, a web database programmer, and a Director of Web Operations. After thirty-four years of gallivanting, I arrived back in Maine with a wife, four children, and two dogs and a cat. A lot happens when you ride away into the sunset.

For many years now, I've been exploring a path that has a great similarity to the one followed by my philosopher mother. I've studied many of the same ancient Christian mystics that she read in her religious quest as an Episcopalian. As I delved into the writings of a broad range of mystics, I discovered what was to become one of my core beliefs—that no one can be closer to a person than the indwelling God. I can say with immense gratitude that I am passionately in love with God.

Partly through my own experience with God, I have developed a profound appreciation for the kind, gentle, compassionate, egalitarian, and respectful love that I feel that God has for each individual.

God is my Great Solace. Deepening my awareness of God's presence and expressing God's love to others are the central goals of my life, both here and in the spirit world. I am grateful that my faith in God and my vision about a world of love have been profoundly informed by the mystics who taught about the indwelling God.

My life now is a tremendously exciting adventure—the mystical search to become resonant with the indwelling God of love and kindness and compassion.

It is a search imbued with daily enthusiasm and joy and the conviction that, as Deepak Chopra wrote in *How to Know God: The Soul's Journey into the Mystery of Mysteries*:

> **God enfolds the whole creation,**
> **not just the nice parts.**

From the Text . . .

The twenty-first century can
indeed become the Age of
Illumination—but it will
partially depend upon each
husband and wife searching
for the higher ground of true
love that is burning in each
person's heart, waiting to
expand and multiply into a
culture of kindness and a
world of peace. Building
marriages of true love will
change the world.

Image Credits

Color images used inside the book have been converted to grayscale and some images (including the cover) have been cropped or modified.

Cover Image
Reflection of white swan on a misty calm pond.
© Hannu Viitanen | Dreamstime.com

Photo of Author with Cup of Tea
by Grace Brown

Photo of Polly Kapteyn Brown
Photographer unknown

Photo of Olga Fröbe-Kapteyn
Used with Permission of the Fondazione Eranos, Ascona, Switzerland

Photo of Geertruida Agneta Kapteyn-Muysken
Public domain. G.A. Muysken, Internationaal Archief voor de Vrouwenbeweging (Amsterdam).
Originally published in: BWSA 2 (1987), p. 95-97.
https://socialhistory.org/bwsa/biografie/muysken.

Photo of Kimmy Sophia Brown
by the author

Photo of Carl Falkenberg Brown
Photographer unknown

Photo of Norman Brown and
the Baroness Helen Dean Falkenberg Brown
by family member

Painting of
Baron Conrad von Falkenberg of Trystorp, Sweden
A copy by Axel Gotthard Smith, Swedish painter (1891–1970)
Original painting by
David Klöcker Ehrenstrahl, Swedish court painter (1628–1698)
Oil on canvas. Owners of both paintings unknown.
http://www.lexikonettamanda.se/show.php?aid=14268

Photo of Jonathan Brown
Photographer unknown

Painting of William Wentworth Brown
by Frederick Porter Vinton, Boston, Massachusetts, USA
Painted in 1902, Oil on canvas, 4' x 5' (framed), commissioned
for $1,600. Used with permission of the Brown Memorial
Library, Clinton, Maine.

Photos of Family at Vaughan Street, Portland, Maine
by family member

Photo of Author on Bicycle at Vaughan Street, Portland, Maine
by family member

Photo of Author at Crescent Beach, Maine
by James Chantler Brown

CPSIA information can be obtained
at www.ICGtesting.com
Printed in the USA
LVHW080706111119
636962LV00012B/5015/P